CANAL
WALKS
MIDLANDS

D1413291

To Mary

who scythed her way through the undergrowth,
stoically resisted the attention of wild beasts
and got thoroughly soaked more than once,
all in the name of a foolhardy husband.

CANAL
WALKS
MIDLANDS

RAY QUINLAN

ALAN SUTTON

First published in the United Kingdom in 1992 by
Alan Sutton Publishing Ltd · Phoenix Mill · Stroud · Gloucestershire

British Library Cataloguing in Publication Data

Quinlan, Ray
  Canal Walks: Midlands
  I. Title
  914.2404858

  ISBN 0–86299–993–6

Library of Congress Cataloging in Publication Data applied for

Typeset in 10/12 Plantin.
Typesetting and origination by
Alan Sutton Publishing Limited.
Printed and bound in Great Britain by
WBC, Bridgend, Mid Glam.

CONTENTS

ACKNOWLEDGEMENTS

This book would have been impossible without the splendid resources of various libraries: communal ownership in practice. Despite chronic underfunding, the information and help received was substantial.

Help and advice on the routes came from: Neil Bough and members of the BCN Society; Roger Cook of the Grantham Canal Restoration Society; Mary Awcock of the Shropshire Union Canal Society; Malcolm Sadler and members of the Stratford-upon-Avon Canal Society; and various employees of British Waterways.

Assistance with the archive photographs came from Roy Jamieson of BW at Gloucester, Lynn Doylerush of the Boat Museum, Ellesmere Port and C. Wilkins-Jones of Norfolk County Council Library & Information Service. Assistance with, though no responsibility for, the author's pictures came from Mr Ilford and Mr Fuji and two, old and increasingly battered, Olympuses fitted with 28 mm and 75–150 mm lenses.

For on the ground assistance during walking trips, thanks to Howard and Jan, Ruth and Rebecca (and Simon) and Paul and Geraldine. Thanks also to Taffy for much of the transportation.

Thanks to Jaqueline Mitchell for helpful comments on the contents and the text.

Many thanks, of course, to Mary – for her patience more than anything else.

Finally, to Humphrey Bogart, whom I've always wanted to be able to thank for something.

LOCATION OF WALKS

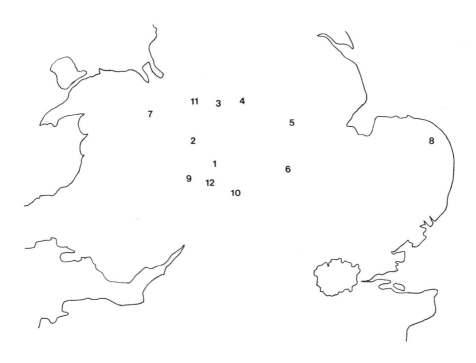

1. Birmingham Canal Navigations at Smethwick
2. Birmingham & Liverpool Junction Canal at Gnosall
3. Caldon Canal at Leek
4. Cromford Canal at Cromford
5. Grantham Canal at Grantham
6. The Leicester Line at Market Harborough
7. Llangollen Canal at Llangollen
8. North Walsham & Dilham Canal at Honing
9. Staffordshire & Worcestershire Canal at Kidderminster
10. Stratford-upon-Avon Canal at Stratford-upon-Avon
11. Trent & Mersey Canal at Stoke
12. Worcester & Birmingham Canal at Tardebigge

KEY TO MAPS

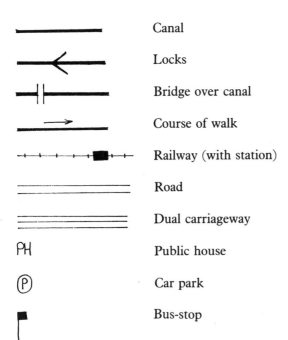

Canal

Locks

Bridge over canal

Course of walk

Railway (with station)

Road

Dual carriageway

PH   Public house

Ⓟ   Car park

▙   Bus-stop

INTRODUCTION

Some two hundred years after the first canal age, Britain has entered a second. Having allowed its waterways to fall into a serious state of decay or even, in many cases, to disappear entirely, the country is now seemingly desperate to clean up its navigable act. The once popular final resting places for old bedsteads, broken pallets and the ubiquitous supermarket trolleys are now being dredged and made into linear water parks, nature trails or public amenity areas. Suddenly, what local authorities once called 'eyesores in need of filling in' are now being described as 'green-fingers into the urban environment'. Councils are putting up signposts and information notices. Canal societies and trusts are opening museums and running boat trips. Enthusiasts, keen enough to forsake an annual sun-drench on the beach in Majorca, are up to their knees in mud restoring lock systems and repairing canal beds. Everywhere it seems, water and boats are being seen where they haven't been seen for years.

Perhaps one of the most interesting things about this renaissance of Britain's canals is that it is only partially for the benefit of those who wish to be waterborne. British Waterways, the guardian of the vast majority of the nation's canal network, admit that although one million people use their lines for boating, some six million use them for walking. Indeed, some canals, such as parts of the Cromford, have been restored with no prospect of any significant boating traffic. The towpaths of the Cromford, and of all the other canals around the country, have become a magnet for walkers seeking to combine a pleasant spot for an afternoon stroll with a place rich in interest and industrial heritage.

What a nineteenth-century boatman would have thought about all this can, of course, only be guessed at. Towpaths were built and maintained not for the benefit of the tourist taking in the scenery but as a part of a means of communication. They were the industrial 'motorways' of the eighteenth and nineteenth centuries. The towpath gave the canal a special advantage. It provided the towing horse with a firm, wide footing. River navigations often didn't possess such luxury and boats were either sailed or bow-hauled by groups of tough, and often rough, men. The towpaths were, therefore, usually as well maintained as the course of the canal itself. After all, if there was no towpath, there was no motive power for the narrowboat on the canal.

Prospects for the towpath changed with the advent of the self-powered narrowboat. From then on it wasn't needed and, in some instances, may even have been removed in order to widen the navigation. Standards of maintenance began to fall and the increased wash from speeding boats caused many sections to erode. Large stretches of many of the country's canals, in this area the northern section of the Stratford Canal, now have no towpath to speak of and are not accessible by foot. And British Waterways aren't required to replace them. Indeed they're not even legally obliged to provide them.

Contrary to popular belief, canal towpaths are mostly not public rights of way. They are technically privately owned land and we are only able to use them through the open-access policy provided by British Waterways. Those canals that weren't nationalized under the 1948 Act, and hence aren't under the control of BW, such as the North Walsham & Dilham Canal, are not open at all and walkers cannot gain access to those lines other than on public rights of way. The permission granted by BW is, of course, welcome by all of us but it raises many a spectre for the future. With increasing economic constraint, BW will, naturally, be forced to investigate ways of maximizing the return from its resources and the popularity of the towpaths will undoubtedly attract attention. It could well be argued that whereas boaters and fisherman have to pay for the privilege of using the waterways, walkers do not. Worse still is the possible position of a privatized BW in which the new owners could remove or restrict access entirely. This would be totally legal given that the routes are not public rights of way.

In the past, the canal companies went to great lengths to ensure that their towpaths were kept off the definitive rights-of-way maps. This was done despite the fact that in many cases the paths had become locally important thoroughfares. This was achieved by periodically closing the path for the supposed reason of maintenance or safety so that the standard definition of a public right of way – that the route has been in uninterrupted use for a period of twenty years – did not apply. Alternatively, notices were erected clearly stating that passage along the path was under sufferance or that access was granted for a particular purpose only. In both cases, it was plain to those using the towpath that it was private land and so could not be declared a public right of way.

Even today, towpaths can be closed without either warning, explanation or the provision of a diversion. The Towpath Action Group has campaigned for some time, for example, over the closure of the towpath on the Ashton Canal in Manchester which has been shut for more than two years while Piccadilly Village has been built. Both the Inland Waterways Association and the Towpath Action Group are seeking to ensure that, where possible, towpaths are declared public rights of way and that the genuine rights of access are maintained. All walkers, especially towpathers, should be alert to these possibilities. Support moves to make your local lines into public rights of way and do report to British Waterways any obstructions and problems along the towpath. In time, it may well be a case of use it or lose it.

The Midland Canals

In so many ways the Midlands are the heart of the English canal network. Many of the earliest and the most successful as well as the most used and battle-scarred navigations are located here. Many of the lines aren't pretty but then they weren't built to be so. They were industrial arteries that fed and thrived on the collieries, quarries and factories of central England. The Trent & Mersey Canal, built under the watchful eye of Josiah Wedgwood, supplied the burgeoning pottery industry around Stoke. Much of Birmingham's industry was deliberately sited next to the city's ever expanding canal network. The Staffordshire & Worcestershire Canal was so busy that it was still able to pay dividends to its shareholders right up to nationalization in 1948, even though trade on most canals had dried up more than fifty years earlier.

It is, however, possible to find peace and solitude on the Midland lines. The once busy, quarry-led, Caldon and Cromford Canals are now splendid rural retreats and the North Walsham and Grantham Canals always were. The Birmingham & Liverpool Junction Canal (or Shropshire Union as it became) passes through some of the remotest parts of the West Midlands while the Llangollen Canal is a stunning construction through some simply wonderful countryside. And who would believe that the Stratford and Worcester & Birmingham Canals are so close to civilization; both make for fine country walking.

Here is just a selection of the canals of the Midlands and, although by no means arbitary, it is strictly a personal choice. Walkers should not ignore the Ashby Canal (near Hinckley and Nuneaton), the surprisingly rural Coventry Canal, the Warwick & Napton Canal (near Leamington Spa), the River Soar Navigation (near Loughborough), the Erewash Canal (near Nottingham) or the various remains of the long-lost lines such as the Leominster, the Oakham, the Shrewsbury, the Derby or the Nottingham Canals. All these are worthy of further investigation and, with the aid of an Ordnance Survey map, can be traced both on paper and on the ground.

As with all personal choices, some people's favourite lines or stretches of waterway may have been omitted. There is also the problem as to what constitutes a Midland canal. The Oxford, for example, runs further north than the Stratford and yet will be included in *Canal Walks: South*; the Trent & Mersey goes as far north as the Macclesfield, even though the latter has been designated as northern. In all these matters, only the author is to blame. I have not tried to be the sage on these matters merely a stimulus. Walking the canals of the Midlands should be an adventure with plenty to see and to discover for yourselves. And it is quite likely that you will find even more than I did and enjoy them every bit as much.

Walking the Towpaths

The walks in this book are all straightforward and require no special feats of strength or navigation. Towpath walks have two great virtues: they are mostly on the flat and they have a ready made, unmistakable course to follow. Getting lost should therefore, in theory at least, be relatively hard. The key problem with towpath walks is that if you want to spend most of the day by the canal, circular routes to and from a vehicle or a particular station or bus-stop become difficult to organize. Many of the walks described within this volume involve walking one way and returning by public transport. This means that you must check the availability of the bus or train before travelling. Telephone numbers are provided for your use and your local library should have the main British Rail timetable.

Walkers should generally plan for 2 to $2\frac{1}{2}$ miles an hour so that stops can be made for sightseeing or a break. Head-down speedsters should easily manage three miles an hour on a good track. You should, of course, add a little time for stoppages for refreshment and add a lot of time if you are accompanied by photographers or bird watchers.

No special equipment or provisions are needed to walk the towpaths of Britain. On a good day and on a good path, any comfortable footwear and clothing will do, and you'll be able to leave the laden rucksack at home. However, for longer walks through more remote country you should be more prudent. Even in a drought, towpaths can be extremely muddy and, from experience, it can not only rain virtually anytime but usually does. Boots and a raincoat of some sort are therefore advisable. Similarly, although pubs and small shops are often fairly common along the way, it may be useful to carry some kind of snack and drink with you.

This book includes sketch maps that show the route to be taken. However, the local Ordnance Survey map will always be useful and the appropriate map numbers and references are provided in each chapter. Again your local library may well have them for loan.

Finally, the dangers inherent in walking along a waterway are often not fully appreciated. Over the 1990 Christmas holiday, three children died after falling into a lock on the Kennet & Avon Canal at Burghfield. Locks are deep, often have silt-laden bottoms, and are very difficult to get out of. Everybody, especially children, should be made aware of this. If somebody does fall in, you should not go into the water except as a last resort. You should LIE on the bank and use something like a coat for the person to grab so that you can then pull them in. Better still, keep children away from the edge.

Otherwise, please enjoy.

1
THE BIRMINGHAM CANAL NAVIGATIONS

The Smethwick Round

Introduction

Ask virtually anybody to say what they know about Birmingham and they will quite possibly tell you that it has more canals than Venice. While this is not the place for a discussion about quantity and quality, it is a remarkable fact which has produced one of the most convoluted waterway systems in the country. To the uninitiated a map of the canals that run around the city, and from there into the Black Country, looks like a dropped plate of spaghetti, randomly arranged and impossibly tangled. To the initiated, however, the Birmingham Canal Navigations, as the canals are collectively known, are an intimate and historic network of waterways with a kind of grubby charm and a lasting appeal.

In the middle of the nineteenth century there were over 160 miles of canals in the BCN. Over the years this has gradually dwindled to about 100 miles of interconnecting waterway made up of a series of individual lines. The earliest of those lines and the main core of the BCN is the Birmingham Canal. This main line runs from Aldersley on the Staffordshire & Worcestershire Canal through Wolverhampton to Birmingham centre at Newhall and Gas Street. Off this line run a series of later canals. From the north-west the first is the Wyrley & Essington (the Curley Wyrley) which runs from Horseley Fields Junction to Brownhills. At Tipton, the Dudley No. 1 Canal goes south-east through the 3,172 yd long Dudley Tunnel to Primrose Hill and on to join the Stourbridge Canal. A little further on, the Netherton branch goes through the 3,027 yd long Netherton Tunnel to the Dudley No. 2 Canal which at one time joined the Worcester & Birmingham at Selly Oak. At Pudding Green, the Walsall Canal winds its way north to reach the W & E at Birchills Junction. From the Walsall at Ocker Hill, the Tame Valley Canal sets off east to Gravelly Hill. Further along, the Birmingham & Fazeley Canal runs from the main line at Farmer's

Bridge to meet with the Tame Valley Canal at Gravelly Hill and then on to a junction with the Coventry Canal at Fazeley Junction. From this, the Digbeth branch joins with the northernmost section of the Grand Union Canal (formerly the Birmingham & Warwick Junction Canal). Although there are numerous other lines and branches, the only remaining section of any length is the Rushall Canal: a north–south line which goes from the Rushall Junction with the Tame Valley Canal, through Aldridge to meet with the W & E at Brownhills.

A walk along any of these canals, through the often derelict industrial parts of an inner city, isn't to everybody's taste but here you will see the last remains of a once busy canal system. With an awareness of the remnants comes an intensity of interest. These aren't pretty lines that look like rivers flowing through attractive countryside. These are canals that have worked for their living and which more often than not show their scars. Towpathers should, therefore, enjoy them for what they are and leave their pretty-view photography for the Llangollen.

History

The thirty thousand people of the small town of Birmingham must have looked eagerly at their Aris's *Birmingham Gazette* in January 1767. Within those pages, a correspondent (a 'well wisher to the town') had written glowingly of the potential for a canal to run from the recently authorized Staffordshire & Worcestershire Canal at Wolverhampton into Birmingham. The letter, promising cheaper coal and other commodities, obviously fell on eager ears for in the following week (28 January) a meeting was held at the Swan Inn to discuss the letter and its suggestion. This meeting decided to ask James Brindley, the engineer of the Bridgewater Canal, to carry out a survey and to make recommendations. To this end, some 165 individuals contributed a guinea each towards the cost. At a follow-up meeting on 4 June Brindley duly reported on a line that went from Newhall in central Birmingham (near Paradise Circus) via Smethwick, Oldbury, Tipton Green and Bilston to Aldersley. It would cost, he said, £50,000, a sum that was easily raised by the following August.

The Birmingham Canal Company was authorized by an Act on 24 February 1768 to build a waterway along Brindley's suggested route with powers to raise £55,000 with an extra £15,000 should it be needed. The new company appointed Brindley as engineer and the work began virtually immediately with Robert Whitworth and Samuel Simcock acting as the great man's assistants.

The first ten miles from Birmingham to the Wednesbury collieries were opened on 6 November 1769. The entire $22\frac{1}{2}$ mile route was completed in 1772 and opened for traffic on 21 September. It was a typical Brindley contour-following canal with twelve locks lifting it up the hill to Smethwick and another twenty taking it down to Wolverhampton and Aldersley. The final cost was over estimate at £112,000 but this included the funds needed to build branches to Wednesbury and Ocker Hill.

Despite the overspending, the line was an immediate success, benefiting enormously from the fact that it passed directly through an area of great mineral wealth and rapidly developing industry. The canal was, virtually from the start, supplying coal, pig-iron, limestone and raw materials to industry, and stone, brick, slate, timber and other cargoes to the town. The Birmingham Canal Company was, however, soon seen to be exploiting the position that they had developed and they came to have a dreadful reputation. They were widely regarded as holding a monopoly on coal supplies and to be 'creaming' the market. This reputation was to be maintained for many years and the company's aggressive, high-handed dismissal of such charges carried through to their future dealings with other canal companies.

With the high profile held by the Birmingham Canal Company and the evident profits to be made, others soon sought similar fortune. The Birmingham & Fazeley Canal was first discussed at a meeting in Warwick in August 1781. The B & F was originally going to run east from Wednesbury via Fazeley to join the Coventry Canal at Atherstone. This was later amended to a line that started in central Birmingham and stopped at Fazeley, where a new stretch of the Coventry Canal would meet it. Another new line from Fazeley to the Trent & Mersey at Fradley would also be built to open a further route to the north. This proposal was warmly supported by the Oxford, Coventry and Trent & Mersey Canal companies all of whom saw potential for business to the east of Birmingham. The Birmingham Company, however, was furious and decided upon 'all possible opposition' to this potential competitor. An unseemly row blundered on for a year and a half before the heavily contested Birmingham & Fazeley Act was passed in June 1783. In 1784, the still antagonistic Birmingham Company solved the issue by simply flexing its financial muscle. It bought its potential competitor and then amalgamated with it to form the Birmingham and Birmingham & Fazeley Company, later renamed the Birmingham Canal Navigations. The new company soon built the Broadwaters Canals (via Ryders Green) as well as the new Fazeley line, which was opened in August 1789.

This growing network of waterways was soon generating considerable business and traffic jams were frequent along the main line. The company felt compelled to make improvements and the engineer John Smeaton was called in to advise. During 1789–90 the summit level at Smethwick was lowered by 18 ft in order to remove six locks. Other locks were duplicated to permit two-way traffic. By 1793, the congestion had eased somewhat and a hundred boats a day were passing along this section of the canal.

Again this success attracted others to enter the navigation business. The Dudley and Stourbridge Canal Companies had, with Thomas Dadford as engineer, built a line from the mines around Dudley to join the Staffordshire &

Worcestershire at Stourton Junction. This had been authorized on 2 April 1776, much to the annoyance of the BCN who feared that its more northerly route to the Staffordshire & Worcestershire Canal was being subjected to a southerly short cut. By 1779, this line from Stourton was open to a point just below the present Blower's Green Locks about a mile south-west of Dudley town centre and the two companies planned to extend their line through a tunnel to join the BCN at Tipton. After several setbacks this extension was started following an Act passed in July 1785. The biggest engineering work on the new line was the 3,172 yd long Dudley Tunnel, a venture that was to take the two companies almost to breaking point. At the beginning of 1787, work had to be stopped when it was realized that the tunnel was out of line. The contractor, John Pinkerton, was relieved of the contract and the company set about the work itself, with Isaac Pratt as engineer. Later he also had to be replaced, this time by Josiah Clowes. It was Clowes who finished the tunnel and continued the new line into Tipton. The new route from Birmingham to the Severn was opened on 6 March 1792 and it did indeed fulfill the BCN's worst fears by providing a much quicker route to Worcester and Bristol. As a result, the BCN proved to be difficult working partners at Tipton Junction, demanding high tolls and being generally uncooperative.

The Dudley company, tired of the pedantic nature of the BCN, sought alternative routes into central Birmingham. With the passing of the Worcester & Birmingham Canal Act in 1791, they decided to build a new line to join the W & B at Selly Oak. This move would allow coal from the Netherton collieries to be taken to markets to the south without entering into BCN waters at all. The W & B were clearly delighted as they too had found dealings with the BCN unrewarding – having been refused access to BCN water at Gas Street. The new Dudley No. 2 Canal, 11 miles long, was opened in 1798. It boasted two tunnels including one at Lappal which was the fifth longest in Britain. It was cut with enormous difficulty, suffered continuously from subsidence and roof falls and was frequently closed for repair. The financial strain of building and maintaining the canal crippled the Dudley company which was eventually absorbed by the BCN in 1846. Lappal Tunnel finally succumbed to its inherent instability and was closed in 1917.

In the north, it was the Wyrley & Essington Company which dared challenge the BCN's supremacy. The W & E from Wolverhampton to Wyrley was opened in 1795 under the direction of William Pitt. This line also proved to be a prosperous one and was extended firstly to Brownhills and then to the Coventry Canal at Huddlesford. This important through route to the Trent & Mersey at Fradley was sadly abandoned in 1954. Several branches were added to the W & E to service the collieries in Cannock and Brownhills. These provided the W & E with a good trade especially when the Black Country pits began to decline.

While the W & E was expanding to the north-west, the BCN was spreading northwards to Walsall. To the outsider, it was an obvious step that an additional link between the two lines should be made. But, typically, the intense rivalries between the companies meant that a junction wasn't built until 1840 when the Walsall Canal was extended via eight locks to Birchills Junction.

Traffic on the BCN during the early nineteenth century continued to increase and with it so did the wealth of the company. By the 1820s, Brindley's main line at Smethwick was again becoming congested and there were continuing water supply problems to the very short summit pound. In a major upgrading of the line, steam pumps were installed to restore lost water, and Thomas Telford was appointed to advise on the condition of the main line. Telford, never a man to do things by halves, modernized the canal in a dramatic fashion between 1825 and 1838. He constructed massive cuttings and embankments to produce a straight, virtually lock-free line from Deepfields to Birmingham that chopped about a third of the distance off the route from Aldersley to Newhall. As the old line remained in use, the improvements also increased the amount of waterway available.

The improvements had a significant impact on both the ease of navigation and on the BCN's finances. They had cost £700,000 and had increased the company's debts to over half a million. This was partly paid off immediately by shareholders or later recovered from them by reducing dividends. But overall, the company was still in a very healthy state with revenue throughout the 1830s and '40s being over £100,000 p.a.

A zinc engraving by L. Haghe, from *c.* 1830, of Telford's fine Galton Bridge which at the time it was built was the largest bridge span over the biggest earthwork anywhere in the world. The scene includes a Pickford's Joey boat and horse underneath the bridge

British Waterways

By this time, however, there was growing concern over the incursion of the railways and in particular the proposed line from Birmingham to Liverpool. The Grand Junction Railway was opened into the city in January 1838 and, in the following November, it was followed by the London to Birmingham line. Perhaps it was this threat, together with the need to build the Tame Valley Canal, that led, in 1840, to the merger of the BCN and W & E. The Tame Valley Canal was built as a bypass for the increasingly congested Farmer's Bridge Locks. Even though the locks were open for twenty-four hours a day and seven days a week, the line along this part of the Birmingham & Fazeley was causing severe traffic jams. The new Tame Valley line was opened in 1844 and ran from the Walsall Canal to the B & F near Gravelly Hill. At roughly the same time the Bentley Canal (which joined the W & E with the Walsall) and the Rushall Canal (which joined the W & E with the Tame Valley) were also built.

By this time, the BCN Company was considering its future in relation to the railways with increasing seriousness. In 1845 the company was adhering to its normal aggressive stance by becoming involved in the construction of a railway between Birmingham and Wolverhampton (the Stour Valley line). But by 1846, when the Dudley Canal Company had been amalgamated into the BCN, the situation had crystallized into one in which the recently formed London and North Western Railway agreed to lease the BCN in exchange for a 4 per cent guaranteed dividend on the shares. The ultimate control of the waterway was thus handed over to railway interests in a rather uncharacteristically timid fashion and the hub of the nation's waterway network had lost its formerly fiercely defended independence forever.

Perhaps contrarily, railway control of the BCN led initially to an expansion in the use of the system. New lines were built, for example the Cannock Extension Canal and Netherton Tunnel (opened on 20 August 1858), and a large number of railway/canal interchange basins were constructed to promote inter-transport traffic. The use of the canals by the railway company resulted largely from the way that Birmingham had developed. Many of the city's factories were built around its canals, did not have access to railway lines and were unlikely to gain access in the future. The importance of the canal infrastructure was therefore considerable and would remain so even when most of the other canals around the country were in rapid decline. In contrast, trade on the BCN continued to grow and by the end of the nineteenth century topped eight and a half million tons p.a., most of it local. But these figures hide the fact that the company was finding it harder to cover its costs and in 1867 it could not pay its dividend from income. In 1868, the railway guarantee was called on and the influence of the LNWR increased still further.

After the turn of the century, the BCN's reliance on local business meant that when the Black Country collieries and mines became exhausted so the trade along the canal declined substantially. Perhaps more seriously, the newer

Joe Taylor at the Island Toll House, Smethwick, in 1940. The toll man assessed the load aboard the passing narrowboat and applied the tolls which were either collected immediately or logged. Sadly, these interesting octagonal toll booths were demolished during the 1950s

British Waterways

factories in Birmingham were built alongside the railways and roads and out of reach of the canal system. Yet even as late as 1949 there was still over a million tons of trade on the line, half of it coal traffic. The BCN continued operating right into the 1960s when nearly a third of a million tons of cargo were moved annually. The canal age only came to an end in Birmingham in 1966 when the coal trade finally stopped. Remarkably, there remained a small amount of commercial traffic into the 1970s and, perhaps even more remarkably, some of it was still horse-drawn. Michael Pearson reports that the last commercial load was of chemical waste taken from Oldbury to Dudley Port in 1974.

As trade declined so some of the less important parts of the network fell out of use and were closed. By 1968, a third of the BCN canals had either been officially abandoned or allowed to fall derelict. In the Transport Act of that year, only the main line and the Birmingham & Fazeley Canal were classified as cruising waterways and were given the official protection of the Act. All the rest were classified as 'remainder' and thus, even today, only survive through goodwill rather than by right. But the West Midlands County Council have recognized the amenity value of the BCN and many areas have been steadily cleared and renovated. There is no greater sign of this than the areas around Gas Street where a number of modern developments have been focussed on the waterway rather than shunning it as they would have done just a decade or two ago. The bulk of the BCN has therefore made it through the worst of times and may, perhaps, be heading towards the best.

The Walk

Start and finish:	Smethwick Rolfe Street BR station (OS ref: SP 022887)
Distance:	4½ miles/7 km
Map:	OS Landranger 139 (Birmingham)
Car park:	There are two signposted car parks near the Smethwick shopping centre off Stony Lane and Church Hill Street
Public transport:	Smethwick Rolfe Street is on the BR main line from Birmingham New Street

Warning: my feet got wetter on this walk than on any other in this book.

Smethwick Rolfe Street station is one stop west of Birmingham New Street. The railway runs parallel to the BCN main line for virtually the whole distance so, if you come that way, it's a good idea to sit on the left-hand side of the train in order to get a good view. Car travellers will not be so blessed.

From the station, cross the road to turn right and then left down North Western Road. This bends left to run for about 150 yd before turning right to go over Brasshouse Lane Bridge. From the bridge, or from the footbridge over the railway nearby, there are excellent views up and down the canals. To the right they head off towards central Birmingham, to the left they go towards Wolverhampton.

Two canals and the remnants of a third can be seen from this spot. The higher waterway is the Old Main Line: Smeaton's adaption of Brindley's original Birmingham Canal. The stretch to the left is the summit level of this line. When asked to improve Brindley's canal in 1790, John Smeaton made a cutting slightly to the south of the then summit level so that the canal could be lowered slightly. It now runs at what is known as the Wolverhampton level of 473 ft above sea level. This new line enabled Smeaton to remove three locks at either end and thus to save both time and water loss. The line of Brindley's original canal is still visible as a ledge which runs about 15 to 20 ft above the present upper waterway.

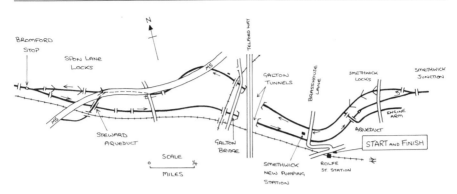

The Birmingham Canal Navigations

When Telford was asked to improve the navigation in the mid-1820s, building technology had moved on considerably. The great man wasn't very flattering about Brindley's canal or Smeaton's renovation of it. 'I found . . . a canal little better than a crooked ditch with scarcely the appearance of a haling-path [towpath], the horses frequently sliding and staggering in the water.' He remedied the situation by building a much straighter line that as far as possible avoided the use of locks altogether. Telford's New Main Line (the lower of the two in front of us) is deeper, with much bolder cuttings, enabling him to take an even lower level than Smeaton; this is the Birmingham level of 453 ft – the same as that in central Birmingham. Telford's line was opened in December 1829 and reduced the travelling distance from Gas Street to Aldersley from 22½ miles to 15 miles and with fewer locks.

Half way across Brasshouse Lane Bridge, pass down a gap in the wall on the left to join the towpath of the Smeaton level. Here immediately on the left is the Smethwick New Pumping Station. Water supply to the short Old Main Line summit was always a problem and, as a consequence, a number of steam pumping stations were built in and around the area to return water lost down the locks. When this engine house was opened in 1892, it contained two steam engines coupled to pumps which lifted water from the New Main Line up to the Old. It continued in use into the 1920s but has since become derelict.

The towpath soon reaches a patch of woodland to the left as the canal bends right. Deep motorbike tyre ruts in the path suggest that some users haven't read BW's carefully considered towpath regulations, nor I suspect have those who have deposited the small mountain of assorted car seats, settees, lumps of metal and planks of wood into the canal itself. Despite this, the line now feels peculiarly rural even if the air smells metallic and fume ridden, and the dull rumble of motor traffic constantly seeks to remind the towpather of the location.

In a couple of hundred yards, the canal reaches Galton Tunnel, a misnomer as the structure is more like an earth bridge. The tunnel dates from 1975 when a new road, The Telford Way, was built to carry traffic from the M5 into Smethwick. The prefabricated concrete cylinder was put into place and then the whole thing covered in soil to make the artificial hill on which the road was built. As far as I know it didn't win any prizes for style but it does have a good towpath all the way through and it eventually opens to reveal the Summit Bridge, built in 1791 and now a scheduled ancient monument. This is closely followed by a blue brick railway bridge.

The canal is now in a modest cutting which still provides a peculiar feeling of isolation from the hubbub that surrounds it. One hundred yards further on to the right is a large bunker-like structure which contains a series of shutes used to load narrowboats with coal. It was built about 1930 and received coal from Sandwell Park and Jubilee collieries via a cable tramway. It was last used in 1970.

The Old Main Line now gradually bends to the left where it suddenly becomes engulfed by the massive concrete pillars that hold the M5 high above the canal. The stark contrast between the gently meandering waterway of the eighteenth century and the harsh, brash motorway of the twentieth is almost shocking in its impact. It's a curiously interesting, if not wholly pleasant, stretch of waterway and not without its hazards. Towpathers will have to stumble over the rubble and mud through here. The situation isn't improved by the constant attention that the flyover seems to need in order to keep it upright.

After surfacing briefly, with the motorway now over to the right, the line passes the high clock tower of Archibald Kendrick & Sons to reach Spon Lane Bridge, an original turnover bridge sadly out of place in this particular location. Cross the canal here and take the right-hand bank which soon winds around to reach Spon Lane Junction. Here a signpost supplied by the BCN Society points off left along the Old Main Line to Wolverhampton via Oldbury. By forking right, we leave the Old Main Line and the M5 and take the line to Bromford. This right turn was formerly a branch off the main line to Wednesbury called the Wednesbury Old Canal.

The first of Spon Lane Locks is immediately on the left. These locks have a single top gate and a doubled bottom. The associated lock bridge is a cantilevered type seen most frequently on the much more rural Stratford Canal. The design allows tow ropes to pass easily through without the need to uncouple the horse. The three Spon Lane Locks take the line down from the Wolverhampton level back to the Birmingham level and are thought to be the oldest working locks in the country. The scene in the early nineteenth century was described by Telford: '. . . at the locks at each end of the short summit crowds of boatmen were always quarrelling, or offering premiums for a preference of passage'. Telford estimated that it was not uncommon for two hundred boats to pass through these locks in a day. Following the completion of the New Main

Line, this situation had apparently changed. John Rickman wrote that the boatmen then met and passed 'with good humour and with mutual salutations'.

After passing a massive car crusher and two more locks, we reach Bromford Junction. Cross the Wednesbury Old Canal via the fine cast-iron bridge, produced at the famous Horseley iron works in Tipton in 1829, to reach Telford's line which now comes in from the left. The two lines join here only to split again about a ½ mile further on when the New Main Line continues on to Wolverhampton while the Wednesbury Old Canal turns northwards towards Walsall.

The island in the middle of the canal to the right is the Bromford Stop. Originally a small toll-house stood on the island from where keepers collected tolls from passing vessels: those going one way passing on one side, those going the other on the opposite. A barrier was held across the waterway to stop the boat. The tonnage carried was then assessed by measuring the depth of the vessel in the water. After the exchange of cash or a chit, the boat was allowed to proceed onwards. Sadly the little hut was demolished in the 1950s and the island is now just another awkward obstacle for passing traffic.

The M5 crosses Telford's
New Main Line on
the Birmingham Canal
Navigations

Turn back almost 180° to continue the walk along Telford's New Main Line. Almost immediately, the straightness and greater width of the newer line is obvious. Telford was particular in avoiding pinch-points at the bridges, a common hinderance in older canals. There are also two towpaths on the Telford line although walkers should stay on this left-hand bank to pass another Horseley bridge.

A $\frac{1}{4}$ mile further on, the canal again passes under the M5, fortunately this time only briefly, and then Steward Aqueduct. This latter structure, built by Telford in 1828, carries the Old Main Line as it swings round from Spon Lane Junction to go south. In building his new line, Telford dug this staggering cutting underneath the old canal thereby enforcing the construction of the aqueduct which was named after a member of the company's committee. The new line is now wedged between the high walls of Chance's glassworks to the left and the railway to the right. For those who might think the area bereft of wildlife, a heron lept into the air and disappeared over the railway wall as I passed here. Two more bridges are passed before we reach a large blue brick bridge, Spon Lane South Bridge.

The line now opens out slightly as Telford's cutting proceeds onwards for about a $\frac{1}{2}$ mile before reaching a dull grey railway bridge, underneath which is the place where shopping trolleys go when they die. Immediately after, however, is the magnificent Galton Bridge. This is Telford at his best. Built in 1829 to carry Roebuck Lane over the new canal, Galton Bridge is 150 ft wide and 71 ft above the canal. When it was built it was the largest single-span bridge over the largest earthwork in the world. Like the lesser footbridges that abound up and down the BCN, it was cast at Horseley works and has recently been sympathetically painted to enhance its fine structure. Its importance has been acknowledged and it is now a Grade I listed building.

The same cannot be said of Galton Tunnel, the mirror image of the one met on the Old Main Line. The only good thing is that we are soon through it and out on to a resurfaced towpath which leads around to the Smethwick New Pumping Station passed earlier. This time we go under Brasshouse Lane Bridge which was built in 1826. From the low level of the Telford canal, it is now possible to see the high retaining wall that holds North Western Road in place.

The line bends slowly to the left to reach another splendid cast-iron structure: the Engine Arm Aqueduct which carries the Engine Arm Canal from the Old Main Line across the New and over to Lime Wharf to the south. The prime purpose of the Engine Arm was to act as a feeder canal from the Rotton Park reservoir (about $1\frac{1}{2}$ miles to the south-east) to the Smethwick summit. The Smethwick engine which did the pumping was built by Boulton and Watt and installed in 1779. It was one of their first and still survives, albeit in the Birmingham Museum of Industry and Science. It is reputed to be the oldest working steam engine in existence. It was Telford who made the arm navigable (so that coal could be delivered directly to the engine site) and who designed the aqueduct. The engine (and another that had been installed later) was removed in 1897. The aqueduct luckily remains and, in its own small way, is every bit as fine as Galton Bridge. Again the paintwork is sympathetic with the structure which has the superficial appearance of the inside of a church. The cast-iron trough which runs across the length of the aqueduct is clearly visible but the design shows how a fairly routine structure can be made beautiful with a little careful effort. If only Telford had designed the M5 flyover!

After the aqueduct, the canal narrows to reach a gauging station similar in theory to the one at Bromford. The only difference is that at this station there are two islands dividing the canal into three. Here the toll clerk measured the height between the water level and the upper side of the deck of the narrowboat (a distance known as the freeboard). From this he was able to work out the weight of cargo being carried and hence the toll that was due to the company. This was done by having previously recorded the unladen freeboard, measured when the boat was first built, and knowing how far the boat sank into the water at different cargo weights.

Further on, eagle-eyed towpathers will have noticed that the embankment to the left has gradually declined. Eventually as we pass under Rolfe Bridge, it disappears altogether and we reach Smethwick Junction where the Old Main Line and the New Main Line merge to head off towards central Birmingham. The two Horseley cast-iron bridges date from 1828 and, like the others on this walk, were assembled on-site on brick abutments. A BCN Society signpost again marks the junction. The installation of these very useful signposts (there are thirty of them altogether) was started in 1983 and has been undertaken by the society with the occasional contribution from a sponsor. The posts were made by the Royal Label Factory at Chipping Norton. It is a sad reflection that these fine posts, purchased by a voluntary society, have been regularly vandalized. Incredibly some have even been sawn off at the base!

We turn left to return to the Old Main Line. This soon reaches Pope's Bridge which carries Bridge Street from Smethwick towards Handsworth. When Smeaton revised the height of the Old Main Line summit, he not only removed three locks at each end but he also built a duplicate set for the three remaining locks at this end. Brindley's set remained in use into the 1960s when they were filled in. Just as you pass under Pope's Bridge, you can see the remnants of Brindley's original line on the right where the entrance to the bottom lock still exists with a reed-ridden side pound and a bricked-up arch in the bridge. On the other side of the bridge, we pass the first of Smeaton's locks and then go on to the next two which take us up to the Wolverhampton level. At the end of the third lock, it is again possible to make out the entrance to the Brindley lock on the other side of the canal. Roughly opposite this lock on the left-hand side is the Engine Arm Aqueduct. If you have time, you can take the left hand bank of the arm round for about a $\frac{1}{2}$ mile to Lime Wharf and a building which was formerly a malt-house.

The final stretch of the walk up to Brasshouse Lane Bridge is now in view. On the right is the site of Smethwick Brasshouse which was established in 1790 and had its own canal wharf. It was later converted into an iron and steel works but was closed in the early 1980s.

Just before passing under the bridge, take the slope to the left which goes up to the road and turn left to reach the railway station and the end of the walk.

Further Explorations

With about one hundred miles of waterway still open for navigation, the BCN has potential for a seemingly endless combination of walks. It has to be said that not all of it makes for particularly attractive scenery but it is all a matter of taste and there is an amazing variety. You can walk through the inner city scrapyard of the Walsall Canal or the open countryside around the eastern end of the Birmingham & Fazeley. You can go through the open tunnel formed by Spaghetti Junction as it rides high above the Tame Valley Canal or the real 3,027 yd long pitch blackness of the Netherton Tunnel on the Dudley Canals. And not only is the choice of view tremendous but from the BCN you can walk to virtually anywhere on the canal system. Go along the Birmingham Canal to Wolverhampton and you can join the Staffordshire & Worcestershire and the Shropshire Union Canals. A walk from Gas Street in the centre of the city will take you immediately on to the Worcester & Birmingham Canal and later on to the Stratford. Take the Birmingham & Fazeley eastwards and you will join the Coventry Canal and then the Trent & Mersey. Go along the Digbeth branch from Aston and before long you'll be able to start a trek to London along the Grand Union.

Despite this huge choice, it's virtually impossible to visit the BCN without visiting the Gas Street Basin and the central Birmingham & Fazeley. For a walk of approximately 2 miles start at New Street station in the centre of the main shopping area. Leave the station to reach New Street where the first of a series of useful signposts points towards the Convention Centre. Follow these signs to Paradise Circus and through Paradise Forum and out towards the Repertory Theatre and the Convention Centre. Turn left here to cross Broad Street and go down Bridge Street. After passing in front of the Hyatt Regency Hotel, you will reach the James Brindley pub and the entrance to the Gas Street Basin.

Originally the main area of wharfage was on the left-hand side of Bridge Street, stretching right over to the BCN's offices – a spot now occupied by Central TV. Gas Street is still the place where the Worcester & Birmingham Canal joins the BCN at a point known as the Worcester Bar. For many years the BCN refused the W & B access to their line and cargo had to be manhandled across the bar which prevented boats from moving between the two canals. Eventually common sense prevailed and the bar was replaced by a lock where passage was possible but where tolls were exacted. Looking from the pub, the W & B is on the left. To see what remains of the bar take the left-hand pathway which leads round the side of the pub and over to the small Horseley iron bridge. The clearly defined remnants of the lock can still be seen from the bridge. This is also a good vantage point for views of the basin as a whole. The extent of recent 'improvements' can be seen here with the old and new sitting uneasily with each other. I, for one, only regret that I didn't see it before. Old timers speak fondly of the atmosphere of the old basin and harshly of the yuppie pub and the brash hotel. It's not exactly unpleasant now. It's simply that it has less authenticity.

Retrace your steps to the pub and take the path which goes left over the small bridge across an ex-factory arm and under Broad Street Tunnel. Shortly the sight of the new Convention Centre hits you. Is there any more extraordinary sight in the British canal network? This architect's view of heaven is juxtaposed with the former working waterway and, across the line, a stretch of scrappy dereliction. Best to walk on quickly to reach Farmer's Bridge Junction. Here a series of lines run off at angles. The first left, under a roving bridge, is the Oozells Street Loop, part of Brindley's original winding main line. Next right is Telford's much straighter New Main Line. We, however, turn right to follow the Birmingham & Fazeley Canal towards Fazeley. Incidentally, after crossing the bridge, it's worth pausing a while to read the interesting and informative notices put up by the Birmingham Inner City Partnership as part of their canal improvements programme.

The city scenery is now more in keeping as you pass under Tindal Bridge to reach Cambrian Wharf, heavily renovated but not unpleasantly so. This was formerly the Newhall Branch Canal that went off right for a $\frac{1}{2}$ mile to Newhall Wharf. The wharf fell into disuse in 1901 and has since been filled in and built on. Another short section called Gibson's Arm also offered wharfage. This area has now been converted into gardens between the new Convention Centre and Paradise Circus.

Bear left to pass a small toll office to reach the first of the highly atmospheric Farmer's Bridge Locks. By means of this flight of thirteen locks, the canal gradually slides down the hill towards Aston Junction. On the way, the intimacy produced by the close crowding of the buildings is awe inspiring. Many of them have their own wharves including covered loading areas. By lock 8, a joint council–company project has produced the Canning Walk on the opposite bank but the most peculiar section is that after lock 9. Here a high-rise office block completely engulfs the canal and lock 10 only to release them into a canyon made up of office blocks on either side of the line.

After passing lock 12, the canal goes through the massive cave that is formed by the railway bridge which carries lines into Snow Hill station. This is followed

An office block engulfs the canal and two of the Farmer's Bridge Locks on the Birmingham Canal Navigations

by the final Farmer's Bridge Lock and Snow Hill Bridge. Here ascend to the road and turn right to follow signs to Snow Hill station and then New Street station to complete the walk.

It is possible to continue for a further 2 miles by going on to Aston Junction and turning right to go along the Digbeth branch. This eventually leads round to the Warwick Bar and the Grand Union Canal. As the GU turns off right continue over the roving bridge to reach the road. Turn right to return to the city centre.

Further Information

The Birmingham Canal Navigations are blessed with a vigorous and enthusiastic society which holds regular meetings and publishes a newsletter. If you wish to join or help or both, you should contact:
    Neil Bough,
    BCN Society,
    60 Tresham Road,
    Great Barr,
    Birmingham,
    B44 9UD.

There are a number of locally available leaflets that describe various parts of the BCN. One set has been produced by the Birmingham Inner City Partnership and the other by the Sandwell Metropolitan Borough Council. Copies of both sets are available from local libraries.

The best guide to the BCN as a whole is:
Pearson, Michael, *Canal Companion Birmingham Canal Navigations*. J.M. Pearson & Associates, 1989.

For historical detail, however, the following are recommended:
Bainbridge, S.R., *The Birmingham Canal Navigations*, vol. 1 (1768–1846). David & Charles, 1974. (NB there is no vol. 2.)
Hadfield, Charles, *The Canals of the West Midlands*. David & Charles, 1969.
Rolt, L.T.C., *Thomas Telford*. Penguin Books, 1958.

2
THE BIRMINGHAM & LIVERPOOL JUNCTION CANAL

Gnosall Heath to Grub Street

Introduction

The Birmingham & Liverpool Junction Canal, or the Shropshire Union as it became, is a thoroughly modern waterway. As an antithesis to Brindley's contour followers that called in at all the local villages, Thomas Telford made the B & LJ as straight and lockless as possible. The aim was simply to produce the fastest practicable route from the city of Birmingham to the River Mersey. As a result, the Shroppie is littered with dramatic embankments and cavernous cuttings, built using techniques that were unknown in Brindley's time and barely achievable in Telford's. Indeed, it may be said that the B & LJ's cut and fill engineering makes it more akin to a modern motorway than to the Oxford Canal or the Staffordshire & Worcestershire.

From Autherley, on the Staffordshire & Worcestershire Canal near Wolverhampton, the B & LJ runs north-west, taking a direct line through the Staffordshire countryside past Brewood and Wheaton Aston. After Gnosall Heath, the canal passes over the Shelmore embankment to Norbury Junction, from where a line formerly ran west to join the Shrewsbury and Shropshire Canals at Wappenshall. The B & LJ, meanwhile, continues briefly into Shropshire and through the 100 ft deep Woodseaves cutting to Tyrley. Here, unusually, are five locks that take the line down to pass Market Drayton and on to Adderley and Audlem. The fifteen locks that constitute 'the Audlem Thick' take the line down 90 ft into the Cheshire countryside. After crossing an aqueduct over the River Weaver, the canal takes a straight course to the outskirts of Nantwich where, near Nantwich Basin, it crosses an aqueduct over the A51 and joins the old Chester Canal. The Shropshire Union now runs past Hurleston Junction (for the Llangollen Canal) and Barbridge Junction (for the Middlewich branch to the Trent & Mersey Canal) and then on for another

16 miles to Chester. From there the Wirral line of the old Ellesmere Canal continues for a further 8½ miles to Ellesmere Port.

The Shroppie is a tricky canal for towpathers. Its straightness and its route through some remote rural countryside puts circular walks or those that use public transport for a return journey virtually out of the question. But the B & LJ makes an excellent long-distance path and, anyway, Telford's massive earthworks are well worth seeing twice.

History

The story of the B & LJ starts in 1824 when Thomas Telford, in making recommendations for the renovation of the Birmingham Canal Navigations' main line, suggested that an improved waterway to the Mersey would increase that company's business to the north-west. With the threat of a railway line between Birmingham and Liverpool hanging over them, the BCN Company grabbed the idea as a way of competing with the new fangled, and as yet largely unproven, mode of transport.

Virtually from the start, the line was established as running from Autherley, on the Staffordshire & Worcestershire Canal near Wolverhampton, to the Ellesmere & Chester Canal near Nantwich. The Chester Canal, a line of nearly 20 miles from Nantwich to Chester, was opened in 1779. The Ellesmere had been started as a much grander venture designed to link the Mersey with the Severn. Such splendid hopes, however, had petered out into a Welsh branch from Hurleston, just north of Nantwich (see the Llangollen Canal), and a northern stretch of 8½ miles from Chester to Ellesmere that became known as the Wirral line. This meant that by 1796 a canal from Nantwich to the Mersey was open but with no southern connection. After the amalgamation of these two companies in 1813, the new Ellesmere & Chester Canal Company actively sought to extend their waterway south and welcomed the promotion of the B & LJ. Naturally, the company hit hardest, the Trent & Mersey, weren't so enthusiastic and responded to the potential newcomer by appointing Telford to upgrade their line with doubled locks and a new Harecastle Tunnel (see the Trent & Mersey Canal).

The new project was widely promoted during the course of 1825 and, in May 1826, an Act was passed to authorize the raising of £400,000 capital with £100,000 in reserve. Thomas Telford was appointed as the canal's principal engineer in what was to be his last major project. A later Act, in 1827, added the Newport branch: a line that went west from Norbury to join the Shrewsbury and Shropshire Canals at Wappenshall.

Even at the time, many people felt that to build a canal from Birmingham to

Nantwich was desperately old fashioned. Indeed, other than the Manchester Ship Canal, which was altogether a different kind of venture, the B & LJ was the last major canal project to be started in Great Britain. Even before the canal was open, the country was well into a new age and was developing a more modern form of long-distance transport. As plans for a railway along a similar route had already been proposed, the lobbying for the B & LJ must have been both intense and highly efficient. We can only imagine the excitement, or maybe it was relief, that was felt by the promoters when so many pledged their support for the new canal in direct conflict with the prevailing mood.

The construction contracts were divided into three areas: Autherley to Church Eaton, Church Eaton to High Offley (just north of Norbury) and High Offley to Nantwich. W.A. Provis, who had worked with Telford on the Holyhead Road, took the middle section and the Newport branch. John Wilson, who had also worked with Telford, this time on the Llangollen Canal, was appointed contractor for the two ends. Alexander Easton was appointed as resident engineer based at Market Drayton.

The route taken by Telford was a bold one. The intention was to shorten the Birmingham to Mersey route both in distance and time and so the course ignored previous canal building concepts of following either the contours or the easiest line. The B & LJ drove across the country on high embankments and through deep cuttings. It was thoroughly modern and inordinately expensive. Work started in the northern section in January 1827. By late 1831, with building work under way all along the line and the northern section nearly ready, the company had spent £442,000 and were forced to apply to the Exchequer Bill Loan Commissioners (an early job creation scheme) for a loan of £160,000 which was to be repaid in three years. Part of the problem was the stiff opposition put up by the local landowners. The company expended some £96,119 in compensation, more than they could possibly have expected.

In 1832, a further £24,600 was obtained from the Exchequer with the hope that this would carry the work through to completion in 1833. But the embankment at Shelmore (near Gnosall) was causing both technical and financial problems. Continuing subsidence meant that a single mile long stretch took some six years to build at a time when pressure to complete the work was tremendous. By 1833, Telford's health was failing fast and William Cubitt was called in to deputize. More and more money was needed to make fast the Shelmore embankment and the Grub Street cutting and when the final stretches were opened on 2 March 1835, the total cost of the canal had risen to £800,000, equivalent to £16,000 per mile, not including any interest arrears. Sadly, Telford, who had died on 2 September 1834 at the age of seventy-seven, did not live to see the completion of his last great work.

As built, the B & LJ was $39\frac{1}{2}$ miles long with twenty-nine locks including fifteen at Audlem. It shortened the route from Birmingham to the Mersey by nearly 20 miles and thirty locks and to Manchester by $5\frac{1}{4}$ miles and thirty locks. Cargo from Birmingham could now reach Liverpool in just forty-five hours.

The Staffordshire & Worcestershire Canal viewed the new line as a major threat to its fortunes and saw an opportunity to obstruct the new line at Autherley Junction. Carriers from Birmingham destined for the B & LJ took the BCN main line to Aldersley, then passed along a ½ mile of the S & W to Autherley where they entered the B & LJ. The S & W complained bitterly that it couldn't afford the excessive water loss that this traffic involved and imposed a crippling toll for every lockful that flowed into the B & LJ. In addition, whenever the S & W ran low, permission to withdraw water was suspended and the B & LJ were forced to buy extra supplies from the Wyrley & Essington Canal (the northernmost of the Birmingham Canal Navigations). Not surprisingly, the B & LJ soon grew tired of these tactics and, in a novel manoeuvre, it released a plan for a mile long aqueduct 'fly-over' from the Birmingham Canal to the B & LJ. The S & W was so shaken that it promptly agreed to reduce the tolls. This successful trump card was used twice more on different issues with similar effect in 1842 and 1867.

But the company was not as successful in many of its other ventures. As would be expected with such a late canal, the B & LJ faced immediate railway

The scene at Norbury Junction in 1905 shows that fishing was as popular then as now although it appears that much less equipment was necessary. The entrance to the Newport Branch is on the right. The craft at the company wharf is said to be the narrowboat *Penguin*

The Boat Museum archive

competition and tolls had to be reduced practically from the start. The Grand Junction Railway, which opened for freight traffic in January 1838, could carry goods considerably faster for roughly the same cost and the B & LJ had to respond in order to gain any traffic at all. This meant that with the high building costs, financial problems plagued the B & LJ from birth. By October 1839, the canal was in dire straits, owing well over £350,000. The situation was made worse by the need to expend even more money to enlarge the Belvide reservoir (on the western side of the canal about $1\frac{1}{2}$ miles north of Brewood). Without it there was not enough water to guarantee traffic flow along the line. A further £20,000 had to be spent before it was open in 1842.

The canal was, however, relatively busy carrying a range of cargo. Along the Newport branch, for example, the canal was conveying iron from the Coalbrookdale area on to the main line and then around the country. From Ellesmere Port, there was a large trade in iron ore, wheat and raw materials. The Llangollen branch brought significant quantities of limestone and lime. Limestone was used extensively in the iron industry in Wolverhampton and lime was becoming an essential 'modern' fertilizer. The canal was also carrying some 140,000 tons of coal p.a. Goods on fly-boats were shipped from the Mersey to Birmingham in just twenty-nine hours, a time achieved by giving them priority over all other traffic and by having teams of fresh horses at roughly 20 mile intervals. By 1842, the profits being made by the carrying companies attracted the B & LJ who obtained powers to start their own carrying company for both cargo and passengers.

But the financial situation remained extremely serious. Revenue along the line reached a peak in 1840 when income was just £30,859. No dividends were being paid and the results clearly demonstrated to all those who said that it was a canal 'white elephant' that they were probably right.

It came as no surprise therefore when, in May 1845, the B & LJ announced that it was to merge with the Ellesmere & Chester Canal and that the resultant Shropshire Union Railway and Canal Company (as the company was eventually renamed in 1846) would, in deference to the inevitable, convert their canals into railways. The company had realized that the innovation started by the Ellesmere & Chester of using steam tugs to pull boat trains couldn't be used on its Welsh lines and would never be cheaper to run than a railway. The decision must have been cemented when their engineer, W.A. Provis, assured them that the cost of converting a canal to a railway was half that of building a railway from scratch. The company would therefore be able to compete with the many lines that were springing up in direct competition with its own canals throughout the north-west. This decision was not met with much enthusiasm by the rest of the canal world. The Staffordshire & Worcestershire Canal, vehemently anti-railway at the time, insisted that a stoppage to any part of the inland waterway would 'cripple the whole system'.

The new SU was unmoved. In the company's prospectus, published in

October 1845, four major railways were proposed: a line that went from Crewe to Nantwich and then along the Llangollen and Montgomery Canals to Newtown and Aberystwyth; a line from Wolverhampton to Nantwich; a line from the Trent Valley to Shrewsbury; and a line from Shrewsbury to Worcester. The proposed capital was £5,400,000 in £20 shares and William Cubitt, Robert Stephenson and W.A. Provis were named as engineers. To extend its activities, the SU incorporated the Shrewsbury Canal and, later, the Montgomery Canal (in February 1847). It also took a lease on the Shropshire Canal (on 1 November 1849). The first railway to be built by the company was not, interestingly enough, on a canal bed but on a line between Shrewsbury and Stafford. This joint venture with the Shrewsbury & Birmingham Railway was chosen as it didn't interfere with any current canal activity and would thus give them a 'feel' for the new business before finally committing them to the proposed conversion.

Despite this apparently vigorous start, the period of renaissance of the SU as a railway company was short-lived. By the autumn of 1846, the newly formed London and North Western Railway, seeing that the SU was about to become a serious threat to its own activities and yet could become an important conduit into non-LNWR areas, offered a perpetual lease to the SU and the SU committee agreed. The canal company was to receive 4 per cent on its existing canal stock until its railways were built and then a rent equal to half the ordinary dividends of the LNWR stock. The canal's debt was to be serviced out of canal operating profits. The Act authorizing this move was passed in June 1847.

By 1 July 1849 (by which time the Shrewsbury to Stafford line had opened), the LNWR had persuaded the SU to give up all thoughts of further railway building in return for having its debt serviced. With this, the company's railway ambitions effectively evaporated for ever.

The SU committee may well have made this decision after having seen that the levels of canal traffic had increased substantially. In 1850, the revenue on the line was over £180,000 with a useful profit and a very vigorous carrying business. It must be said that the interest on the company's debts was still £34,473 p.a. and that the SU never earned enough to cover this figure in any year after 1850, the balance being paid by the LNWR. But dividends were paid and, with the LNWR lease, prospects must have appeared reasonable. Only later did the increasing railway competition (from lines which at one time the B & LJ itself had intended to build) make itself felt. From an operating surplus of £45,000 p.a. in the late 1840s, profits dropped to around £11,000 by the late 1860s even though the level of receipts was similar. The SU had been forced to accept lower tolls in the face of railway competition. An agreement with the Great Western Railway for example forced canal rates to below those of the railway for traffic to Llangollen, Ruabon and Chirk. At this time, most of the company's income was, in fact, coming from its canal carrying business rather than from tolls; in 1870 the company operated some 213 narrowboats (of which about a third were employed carrying iron ore or manufactured products) and by 1889 it operated 395. By the end of the century, the company's own carrier was handling over 70 per cent of the trade along the line.

The gradual decline in trade was perhaps inevitable although in the 1890s, with the construction of the Manchester Ship Canal, a brief respite in the downward trend was felt. At that time, the company built new quays, improved facilities and considered the possibility of widening the SU main line to Autherley. The cost was estimated at almost £900,000. Although some minor improvements to a number of wharves were undertaken, the line was not substantially altered and the widening scheme was quietly forgotten.

The new century started with some modest operating profits but, by the time of the First World War, the canal as a whole was running at a loss and the LNWR appeared to lose interest. After the war, the canal began to sustain large losses and the LNWR insisted on economies. On 1 June 1920, the SU

Cadbury's had a fleet of seventeen boats that brought milk from farmers along the canal to Knighton where it was processed and then shipped on to the chocolate factory at Bourneville. This photograph of horse-drawn boats arriving at Knighton was taken in the 1920s
The Boat Museum archive

announced that it was to give up the carrying business that still ran some 202 boats up and down the line. The company also reduced its maintenance effort and closed the locks at weekends. This action reduced the losses from £98,384 in 1921 to £26,473 in 1922 but it was clearly a retrograde step for a working canal. At the end of 1922, the SU company was absorbed by the LNWR which in turn was itself absorbed into the London Midland & Scottish Railway the following year.

In 1929, the SU carried 433,000 tons of cargo but by 1940 this was down to 151,000 tons. The LMS did nothing to encourage traffic along the SU and the lack of maintenance must have acted as a positive discouragement. Road transport was by then becoming the main threat, being both easier and cheaper. Although a widening scheme for the main line was again considered in 1943, it was inevitable that in an Act of 1944 the entire lengths of what today are known as the Montgomery and Llangollen Canals were abandoned (although the Llangollen line was maintained as a water feeder for a reservoir at Hurleston). The last commercial traffic to run along the SU main line came in the form of oil and tar boats from Stanlow near Ellesmere Port to Oldbury in the Black Country. At one time, this trade alone took one thousand boats a year and they were horse-drawn into the 1950s. But by 1957–8, the trade had all but stopped and, although a small amount of traffic continued into the 1960s, the commercial life of the canal was effectively over.

The SU main line was never in the same kind of danger of imminent closure as many of the nation's canals. Even in the Report of the Board of Survey to the British Transport Commission in 1955, the line was deemed worthy of retention. But true safety only came in 1968, when the main line, together with the Llangollen Canal, was classified as a cruiseway under the Transport Act. Since then the line has been gradually improved into the popular cruising route that it is today.

The Walk

Start:	Gnosall Heath (OS ref: SJ 820203)
Finish:	The Anchor Inn, near Grub Street (OS ref: SJ 774256)
Distance:	5 miles/8 km each way
Map:	OS Landranger 127 (Stafford & Telford)
Return:	Along canal
Car park:	On street at Gnosall Heath near The Navigation pub
Public transport:	Happy Days buses go to Gnosall Heath from Stafford (which is about 6 miles to the east) where there is a BR station. For bus enquiries telephone: (0785) 74231

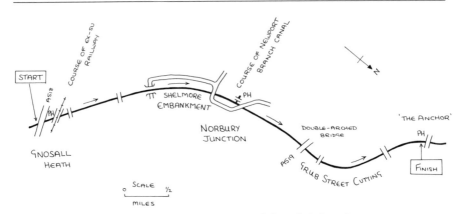

START

COURSE OF EX-SU RAILWAY

A518

PH

GNOSALL HEATH

TT SHELMORE EMBANKMENT

COURSE OF NEWPORT BRANCH CANAL

PH

NORBURY JUNCTION

DOUBLE-ARCHED BRIDGE

A519 GRUB STREET CUTTING

N

'THE ANCHOR'

PH

FINISH

SCALE 0 ½

MILES

The Birmingham & Liverpool Junction Canal

There is no public transport from Gnosall to The Anchor Inn. Towpathers therefore have to find somebody nice enough to pick them up from The Anchor Inn or befriend a fellow towpather so that they can perform a two car trick. The only other alternative is simply to turn round and walk back. Luckily, this stretch of canal is so pleasant that this latter option is no hardship. In addition, if you start out in mid-morning, then the pub can serve its wonderful Wadworth's 6X to you so that you won't notice that you've seen all the scenery before.

The walk starts by The Navigation which is on the western outskirts of Gnosall Heath on the A518 Newport to Stafford road. Take the path which runs down the right-hand side of the pub to walk on the left-hand bank of the canal. You may not wish to know that Gnosall Bridge is reputedly haunted by the ghost of a man who drowned in the canal in the mid-nineteenth century.

The towpath shortly passes a map of the village and some mooring spaces before bending gently left to go under a former railway line. This line is significant because it was the SU's one and only venture into railways before being bought off by the London and North-Western Railway. The line ran from Stafford to Shrewsbury and opened on 1 June 1849. After the rail bridge, the canal enters a small cutting and becomes delightfully peaceful and relaxing. At the next bridge (No. 36), the deep rope cuts in the bridge metals confirm just how busy the line must have been at one time.

At the end of the cutting, the scenery ahead opens out and the canal stretches directly across the landscape, more like a Dutch dyke than an English waterway. The line is held high above the farmland on either side and shows how far Telford had moved on in terms of engineering expertise and ideas from Brindley just fifty years before. Brindley would presumably have locked down here by, say, two locks, possibly adding half an hour or so to the journey time. However, such exposed embankments can be a problem in the face of a gale. As

Tom Rolt found, forward progress can be virtually impossible in some conditions when it is easier just to switch off the engine and sit it out.

After passing an old B & LJ milepost (not a SU one), the canal goes under bridge 37 and on to the start of the Shelmore embankment, announced by the positioning of a massive stop gate on the canal near a small fishing hut. Within a few yards, it becomes clear that the land to the left has fallen away and the canal is now riding high above it on a massive embankment. Indeed, almost unnoticed, the line runs over a minor road by means of a small aqueduct. The canal channel is now concrete lined, a move which only hints at the problems that the B & LJ had with the canal during the construction of this section.

It was never Telford's intention to build such a vast embankment here at Shelmore. Originally, the canal was to run on the level along a line to the east of its present route to take a more direct course from Grub Street to Gnosall. However, Lord Anson refused to allow the company to make a cut through his game reserves in Norbury Park. He claimed that the building of the line and its operation would disturb his fowl and the company was forced to move the canal westwards. To retain height (and hence avoid a sequence of locks), Telford designed an embankment, a mile long and 60 ft high: the Shelmore Great Bank. If you look at the local OS map, the preferred course can be easily traced as the current line makes a sudden and rather awkward westward 'lean' away from Norbury Hall.

The construction of the embankment, under contract to W.A. Provis, began in June 1829 and at both ends. Four hundred men and seventy horses were in action piling up the spoil that was being extracted from the Grub Street and Gnosall cuttings. By July 1830, some half a million cubic yards of soil had been moved to the site but, by the following winter, the embankment was still only a quarter of the desired height. More importantly, it was subsiding. Telford promptly concluded that the problem was with the material they were using and ordered that only sandy soils could be used to build the embankment. This, he said, would be more reliable and he confidently predicted that the works would be ready by the autumn of 1832. By July 1832 he had changed his mind. The embankment, although nearly at full height, was still slowly slipping into the valley below. In August, the gradual slide stopped and a rapid one began. Eight hundred yards of earthworks, half the total length, collapsed. It was clear that the Shelmore embankment was about to become the Shelmore embarrassment.

The situation was not helped by the seventy-five-year-old Telford's failing health. The great man was often simply unable to provide the help and guidance that was necessary. Indeed, it was Alexander Easton who, in the following winter, had to report that, although 300 yd of embankment had been virtually finished, the rest was still slipping. In February 1833, William Cubitt was asked to deputize for the ailing Telford. Cubitt approached the problem with a good degree of self-confidence and recommended that hardcore be used to form a firm base on the bank. By May, the company was adding some 40,000 cubic yd of

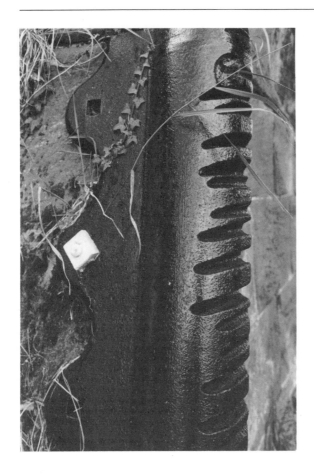

Rope-wear marks on
Machins Barn Bridge near
the Shelmore embankment

hardcore a month to its moving hillside. This they did until January 1834 when
Cubitt was, finally, able to report that the line was nearly ready and that the
puddled bed was virtually complete. Although he added that there were still
signs of shifting along some stretches, there must have been a feeling that the
trauma was over at last. History does not recall a meeting with Lord Anson
when Cubitt and Telford visited the embankment in March 1834, but presumably some wrath must have been vented on the man who had forced them to
construct an otherwise totally unnecessary earthwork simply in order to keep
the game happy.

In May, the embankment slipped again and when Telford died on 2 September, the Shelmore embankment was still not passable; his final great engineering
work remained as two unconnected halves. Cubitt was forced to breach the slide
and to continue adding hardcore. Finally, on Monday 2 March 1835, the first
traffic went along the line. Although only a single boat's width, it was passable.

By July Cubitt was able to report that the line had been completed to full width. It had taken six years to build.

This story of near disaster for the B & LJ company is hard to credit when one looks at the scene today. Shelmore Wood now covers both banks and one would be excused the thought that the canal is one of Brindley's running around a perfectly natural hillside, such is the air of permanence and solidity that it exudes. Only the concrete channel and the history tell us otherwise.

After another milepost, the canal bends around to the right, straightens to pass some moored vessels and arrives at Norbury Junction. Norbury is now a busy little canal centre where British Waterways have an office (responsible for the maintenance of the canal from Autherley to Audlem) and there is a boatyard, a wharf with an old crane, a pub (Junction Inn), a shop and a café. The small chimney stack is all that remains of the steam engine which used to drive the workshop machinery. It's a pleasant spot and suitable for a brief rest before continuing onwards.

Norbury became a boating centre because at one time the Newport branch canal ran from here via a set of locks called the 'Seventeen Steps' to Newport and then on to Wappenshall. There it joined the Shrewsbury Canal and thus the Shropshire and Donnington Wood Canals. This, of course, gave the B & LJ access to the industry around Coalbrookdale and the line was an important conduit for the iron from the area to the rest of the country. The branch was just over 10 miles long and was opened in March 1835. The line was still carrying a small amount of traffic in 1943 but was abandoned as part of the infamous Act of 1944 which put paid to a number of canals owned by the LMS (including the much lamented and soon to be restored Montgomery). The line has since been filled in, built upon and generally neglected. The remains can be seen by walking up to the roving bridge which passes over the former entrance and looking left. The scene may appear to be beyond redemption but the Shropshire Union Canal Society haven't given up all hope and are reportedly undertaking a preliminary feasibility study on the restoration of the branch.

After passing over the bridge and by the Junction Inn, would-be shoppers can cross the next bridge to the small store. Those who wish to can continue on under the bridge (past the stop planks to protect this side of the Shelmore embankment) and into a straight length of canal that appears to be heading directly for a wooded hillside.

Almost imperceptibly, the trees on either side of the canal get taller and it's not until you're some way in that you realize that you've entered another cutting. This is the Grub Street cutting and the site of more headaches for the contractor W.A. Provis. The hill is composed of a friable rock that alternates with beds of clay which crumble when dry and act as a lubricant when wet. Almost from the start of building in 1829, men were employed virtually continuously to clear up the earth slips that plagued the cutting. The worst slip was in May 1834 when 10,000 cubic yd of marl and rock came down to block the

High Bridge in Grub Street cutting on the Birmingham & Liverpool Junction Canal

canal completely for about 60 yd. The only answer was to take the sides further back from the waterway. Similar problems were had at the Woodseaves cutting which is about 8 miles to the north near Tyrley. Grub Street cutting is approximately 80 ft deep and 2 miles long. The depth isn't fully appreciated until the canal reaches the A519 road bridge (No. 39 'High Bridge') which is a curious double-arched affair with an old-fashioned telegraph pole stuck half-way up. It's a strange landmark but oddly memorable. It is also said to be haunted by a black monkey, all that remains of another long-drowned boatman.

Bridge 40 (a footbridge) is nowhere near as interesting but by now the canal is deep into the cutting. The Anchor Inn is about a mile and a quarter away and we walk through a waterway chasm before reaching bridge 41. From here our walls begin to subside and a notice brings our attention to the proximity of the pub.

Just before bridge 42, a gate leads off the towpath and into the beer garden. The Anchor Inn has been known as the New Inn and the Sebastopol but has always been a peculiarly canal-locked hostelry. At one time the pub had its own stables so that hospitality could be offered to the horses as well. Thomas Pellow and Paul Bowen describe evenings in the pub as well as the extraordinary story of Lily Pascall who ran the place from the turn of the century into the 1960s.

Probably nothing too extraordinary will happen to you while you're here but you may be lucky enough to meet the kindly soul who is picking you up or you will have a chance for some R and R before returning to Gnosall.

Further Explorations

The lack of public transport along the B & LJ suggests that one of the best ways for towpathers to see the line is to make it into a long-distance path. With a full length from Autherley to Nantwich of 39 miles, three days and two nights are sufficient for a steady amble along the line.

Day one starts at Autherley Junction (OS Landranger 127, ref: SJ 902020). From Wolverhampton central bus station, take the West Midlands Transport bus 504 or 505 to the corner of Oxley Moor Road and Blaydon Road. Take a lane which runs past the waterworks to the Water Travel boatyard. This provides access to the canal and the towpath at bridge 1 close to the stop lock which controlled water flow from the Staffordshire & Worcestershire Canal.

Having swallowed deeply, towpathers can now put their best foot forward with the hope of reaching the Hartley Arms at Wheaton Aston for lunch (about $7\frac{1}{2}$ miles). The morning will have taken in the splendid Avenue Bridge near Brewood (pronounced brood) as well as the Stretton aqueduct which takes the canal over the A5. The pub is close to the canal on the left-hand side not long after Wheaton Aston lock, the first after the Autherley stop lock. After 13 miles, you reach Gnosall Heath (turn off at bridge 35 when you reach The Navigation) which is a convenient place to aim for the first night. You will however have to take a bus into Newport for accommodation. Check with the bus company for times (0785 74231). Accommodation in Newport includes the Bridge Inn (0952 811785) and Norwood House (0952 825896).

Day two follows the course of the main walk and then goes beyond to the Wharf Inn at Shebdon. The afternoon takes in the peculiarly misplaced factory at Knighton (an ex-Cadbury's milk plant) and then the chasm-like Woodseaves cutting: 100 ft deep and yet another crumbly problem for the hapless Provis and the long-suffering British Waterways. After the five locks at Tyrley, the sizeable Market Drayton Wharf follows within 1 mile. Turn left at the bridge which carries a major road into the town centre (about a $\frac{1}{2}$ mile). Market Drayton accommodation includes the Corbet Arms (0630 2037). You have now done 26½ miles.

The morning of day three is a time for locks. A steady down hill walk should pass seventeen of them before reaching the Bridge Inn next to the canal at Audlem (32½ miles). The final afternoon crosses the Weaver Aqueduct on through the Cheshire countryside to an aqueduct which goes over the A51. Here turn right to take the main road into Nantwich. The town centre is about a ¾ mile from the canal and proffers trains to Crewe and Shrewsbury (enquiries to 0270 255245) as well as a range of buses (0270 212256).

Good luck.

For those with less ambition, a short (4½ mile) walk from Tyrley is worthy of a warm summer's day. Tyrley is signposted along a minor road off the A529 just to the south of Market Drayton. There is a small canalside car park next to the bridge at Tyrley Wharf. Here are some fine Telford-designed buildings (including a lock-keeper's house, a warehouse and other cottages), all of which date from the late 1830s. Here also is a series of five locks (four to the Market Drayton/northern side), the first going north for about 17 miles. Turn right to take the right hand bank past the top lock. Within a short distance, the canal starts to become enclosed by the magnificent Woodseaves cutting. A mile long and, in places, nearly 100 ft deep, Woodseaves typifies Telford's modern approach to canal building. As at Grub Street, landslides were the plague of contractor William Provis' life and still are a problem for British Waterways. A report to BW, made in the autumn of 1990, confirmed that there were continuing stability problems caused by water draining from the sandstone bedrock into the alternating layers of mudstone. This leads to the mudstone slipping and causes the walls of the cutting to sag and collapse. At the time of writing BW are contemplating a major (and expensive) project to secure the walls and prevent any further landslips. From a purely selfish point of view, the towpath through the cutting can also suffer and it's certainly the only one in this book that sports a healthy growth of duckweed.

As at Grub Street, part of the magnificence of the cutting are the bridges and the third bridge from Tyrley, known as High Bridge for fairly obvious reasons, is the best of all. This must be the most outstanding accommodation bridge (a bridge built simply to enable a farmer to pass from one part of his land to the other) in the country. After passing under the next and last bridge in the cutting, the view opens out and the towpather reaches Goldstone Bridge and Wharf where the Wharf Tavern offers a canalside garden, bar foods and drinks: all to be enjoyed before the gentle stroll back to Tyrley.

Further Information

The Shropshire Union together with the Llangollen Canal and the Montgomery Canal are all very ably supported by members of the Shropshire Union Canal Society Ltd. Their address is:

Membership Secretary,
'Oak Haven',
Longdon-on-Tern,
Telford,
TF6 6LJ.

The society is currently engaged in restoring the Montgomery Canal and is investigating the possibility of reopening the Newport branch. All these issues are discussed and news updated in the society's magazine *Cuttings*. New members are, of course, always made welcome.

An excellent history and guide to the Shropshire Union Canal as a whole is:
Pellow, Thomas and Bowen, Paul, *The Shroppie*. The Landscape Press, 1985.

The history of the B & LJ, along with the rest of the canals that make up the Shropshire Union, can be traced through the chapters of:
Hadfield, Charles, *The Canals of the West Midlands*. David & Charles, 1969.

If a fan of Tom Rolt's highly readable style, then a good account of the trials and tribulations of Thomas Telford's last great venture can be found in:
Rolt, L.T.C., *Thomas Telford*. Penguin Books, 1958.

Those considering the long-distance route might find the following of interest:
Morris, Jonathon, *The Shropshire Union. A towpath guide to the Birmingham & Liverpool Junction Canal from Autherley to Nantwich*. Management Update Ltd, 1991.

3
THE CALDON CANAL
Leek to Cheddleton

Introduction

It's hard to believe that the quiet woodlands around Cheddleton are so close to the heaving civilization of the Potteries. You can almost hear the boat crews, who have struggled up from Etruria, sigh with relief as they reach Hazlehurst Junction. There they enter an altogether different world. It's not that the area is without its industrial history, there are remnants of a busy past all the way from Cheddleton to Froghall, but, from Hazelhurst on, nature has regained its rightful place. This is a countryside of rolling hills and abundant wildlife that belies its proximity to the five towns.

The Caldon's $17\frac{1}{2}$ miles start at Etruria where the branch leaves the summit pound of the Trent & Mersey Canal from a spot close to Etruscan Mill and Stoke Top Lock. After winding around the town of Hanley, with its working and historic potteries, the canal reaches the villages of Foxley and Milton and then Engine Lock, so-called because it was formerly the site of a beam engine used to drain the local colliery. A little further on, the feeder from Knypersley reservoir enters and a mile or so further on boats pass through the five Stockton Brook Locks into the Caldon summit pound. At the top level the line passes Endon Basin, now used as a mooring place by the Stoke-on-Trent Boat Club, and skirts around the village of Endon to reach Park Lane Wharf and the Hazlehurst Junction. Here the Leek branch turns right to cross the main line a little further on by means of Denford (Hazlehurst) Aqueduct. The branch then takes off to the north-east to ride high on the hillside and through Leek Tunnel, only to come to an end about a $\frac{1}{2}$ mile outside Leek. Meanwhile, the main line descends by three locks to go under Denford Aqueduct and on to Cheddleton with its fascinating Flint Mill Museum. From Cheddleton the canal makes its way into increasingly remote country. After Oakmeadow Ford Lock, the line joins the River Churnet for about 1 mile. River and canal separate again at Consall Forge, once a busy industrial centre, and move on to Froghall. The canal goes through a short tunnel and past the former entrance of the Uttoxeter Canal to come to a complete stop at Froghall Basin. This once frenetic wharf with its historic lime kilns is now, perhaps rather ignominiously, a picnic site.

Although the Caldon has its origins as a highway for the quarries of the area, it now has a wonderfully tranquil and relaxing atmosphere. Use it as the natural antidote to the Trent & Mersey.

History

Even before the Trent & Mersey Canal had fully opened, the possibility of a branch line from Stoke to Leek was being considered. Indeed it was the Caldon Canal that finally laid James Brindley to rest. In September 1772 Brindley had been surveying the route of the proposed canal at Ipstones, between Leek and Froghall, when he had been soaked to the skin during a thorough downpour. The oft-told story now relates that he then slept in those still wet clothes, caught a chill and finally succumbed on 27 September 1772. With him, for a while at least, went any thoughts about the proposed branch. However, one plan that was circulating at the time was for a very narrow canal that used five ton tub boats in place of narrowboats and inclined planes instead of locks.

It wasn't until November 1775 that Josiah Wedgwood revived the idea and then it wasn't Leek that was his target. This time, it was the potentially lucrative Caldon Low limestone quarries that attracted the entrepreneurial eye. The quarries, owned by the Earl of Shrewsbury, were a few miles east of Froghall (OS Landranger map 119, ref: SK 080485) and, according to John Sparrow, clerk to the Trent & Mersey company at the time, they had an 'inexhaustible fund of Limestone'. Hugh Henshall, Brindley's brother-in-law, surveyed the line and prepared an estimate. The branch was to run 19¼ miles from Etruria via Hanley and Norton to Cheddleton from where 'a railed way' was to be made for the carriage of coal, stone and other goods from the canal to a place called 'Sharpecliffe'. Another length of canal then ran from Sharpecliffe to the Caldon Low quarries. The proposed line would cost exactly £23,126.

Although the quarries offered the potential for more traffic along the line, from some accounts, the T & M's main interest in developing the Caldon Canal was in gaining access to additional water supplies for the main-line summit pound at Etruria. The need for water, described as insatiable by some authors, was stressed by John Sparrow, who clearly saw the Caldon as being able to produce 'a plentiful supply'.

On 12 February 1776, the T & M submitted a petition to Parliament to build the Caldon branch. There were, of course, objections. The millowners at Cheddleton feared loss of water to their works and filed a counter petition

Froghall Wharf was the terminus of the tramways from the Caldon Low limestone quarries and where, as this 1905 photograph shows, narrowboats were loaded for subsequent transport along the canal

Dr J.R. Hollick, The Boat Museum archive

against the proposed line. The proprietors of the T & M were clearly not the kind that were ruffled by challenges of this nature. Their response, on 18 April 1776, was to expand their original proposal with a continuation of the line through to Froghall via Consall. From there, they said, rail lines would go up to the quarries at Caldon Low. As the vast majority of the landowners were in favour of the line, the Act was passed without too much fuss on 13 May 1776. Funds of £25,000 were authorized, a sum which was raised through various loans taken on the credit of the tolls. Three colliery owners from Froghall alone contributed some £5,000. The tolls on the new branch were to be 1½d. per ton per mile for coal, stone, timber and other goods.

In order to guarantee the use of the canal, the company signed contracts with the quarry owners many of whom were already involved with the T & M. The contracts stipulated the amount of stone, gave the right to the T & M to operate the quarries itself if insufficient was delivered, detailed the tolls, and committed the T & M to building branch railways from the canal to the quarries.

There appears to be some confusion about when the Caldon branch opened to traffic but tolls are recorded as being received from Christmas 1778 onwards. The completed canal was just over 17 miles long and cost approximately £23,560. Originally there were fifteen locks with eight uphill and seven down.

This number was later increased to seventeen. The first horse-drawn railway to the quarries from Froghall was opened in about 1779. It started from Froghall terminus (on what is now the Cheddleton side of Froghall Tunnel) by the original kilns on the north side and ran up Shirley Hollow along the Shirley Brook to Shirley Common. This tramroad clearly wasn't the most reliable available and was described as being 'laid and placed in a very inconvenient course and direction' and had 'not answered all the good ends and purposes thereby intended'. As a result additional funds were raised in 1783 to improve matters. As part of these works, the canal at Froghall was extended by 530 yd through a 76 yd tunnel to a new basin. The new railway ran about 3 miles up Harston Wood and then turned right beyond the Harston Rock and over Cotton Common to the quarries. This new work cost £2,671.

By March 1785, the T & M had further developed its Caldon branch by building warehouses, reservoirs for yet more water (Stanley, Knypersley and Bagnall) and new railway lines at a cost of £6,000. The route of the railway was further revised in 1802, this time with John Rennie as engineer. The new line was a double track of flanged plateway that was spiked to stone blocks. It rose up the 649 ft of hillside on five inclined planes using horse power: one horse to twelve wagons.

In March 1797, the company decided to realize its original ambition and obtained an Act to make a branch from Endon to Leek. The prime rationale was not in the likely traffic that this would generate but was related to the additional supply of water from a proposed feeder reservoir at Rudyard Lake (2 miles north-west of Leek). The plan was initially obstructed by the Chester Canal Company who feared, apparently, that the T & M was aiming to 'lay hold of all the Supplies of Water in the Country'. The Leek branch, which had been surveyed by Hugh Henshall but was engineered by John Rennie, was $2\frac{3}{4}$ miles long and forced an alteration to the summit of the Caldon branch. The top pound was originally between the Stockton Locks and Endon (Park Lane). In the new layout, the locks at Endon were removed and the summit extended along a wholly new cut to Hazlehurst where the junction with the Leek branch was constructed. The new branch was fully open in 1802.

It was also in 1797 that the company obtained an Act to continue its line beyond Froghall to Uttoxeter, a distance of $13\frac{1}{4}$ miles. It is said that the main purpose for building the extension was to defeat the projected Commercial Canal, a proposal for a broad navigation from the Mersey along the Grand Junction to London. This direct line would have been a major competitor to the T & M and the company was keen to undermine the new venture wherever possible. Although there may have been this covert *raison d'être* behind the proposal, the Uttoxeter Canal was still seen as having plenty of scope for new business with the main trade coming from the collieries at Cheadle and Kingsley Moor and the copper and brass works at Oakamoor and Alton.

The project met immediate problems when the Earl of Shrewsbury and the

Cheadle Brass Company objected to possible loss of water to their wire mill. Because of this the work was delayed while an answer to the problem was sought. After toying with the idea of building a railway instead, the company decided to start on the new canal while the negotiations continued. This it did in 1807 with John Rennie as engineer. By August 1808, the line reached Oakamoor where work stopped while the agreement on how to proceed past Alton Wire Mill was finalized. With a decision to build a new weir and pond for the mill, work was restarted and the line finally completed on 3 September 1811. The opening of the canal was received in Uttoxeter with a 'great demonstration of joy by the inhabitants'. Guests received a 'cold collation' as well as speeches, toasts and songs, including one specially written for the occasion. The 'poor' received the benefits of two roast sheep and a quantity of bread and ale.

The Uttoxeter extension had seventeen locks, a 40 yd long tunnel at Alton (near the now (in)famous towers) and an iron aqueduct over the River Tean. Such was the enthusiasm engendered by the new line, that imaginative plans were brought forward including one that continued the canal to Burton-on-Trent.

In 1836, the company obtained an Act which allowed it to widen and straighten a section of canal between Oakmeadow Lock and Flint Mill Lock near Consall Forge. Further improvements to both the canal and the tramways were made during the next five years, including a major rebuilding of the Hazlehurst Junction which improved traffic flow considerably. But in 1846 the North Staffordshire Railway (NSR) took over the Trent & Mersey Canal Company, a move that would normally be considered to be the middle of the end. In one way it was. The Uttoxeter extension, which had fulfilled its purpose of defeating the Commercial Canal, was losing about £1,000 p.a. and was promptly closed. The Churnet Valley Railway line (seen as one section of a route from Manchester to London) was built partly on its bed. However, the commitment of the railway company to the rest of the Caldon Canal was as positive as ever. In 1849 the NSR installed a new $3\frac{1}{2}$ ft gauge cable-drawn railway from Froghall to the Caldon limestone quarries and, by the 1860s, a recently discovered band of haematite was producing 400,000 tons of iron ore p.a., about half of which went down the canal.

Such activity was not to last forever. Within a further twenty years, the original quarries were beginning to be worked out and new areas were being opened away from the tramroad and towards Waterhouses (half way between Leek and Ashbourne). It was now far more convenient to move the main quarry terminus further towards Stoke. Endon Basin, a $\frac{3}{4}$ mile from Stockton Locks, was therefore built as a transfer point for limestone brought over from the quarries by rail. By July 1905 a rail link from the new Leek-Waterhouses line was opened to serve the new workings and there was a substantial reduction in canal traffic. In 1920 a series of events effectively finished the line off: the Brunner Mond works at Sandbach, one of the principal users of canal-borne limestone, was closed; a serious landslip occurred on the canal near Froghall; and, on 25 March 1920, the cable line was shut. Transhipment at Endon Basin finally stopped about 1930 and from then on the Caldon Canal was hardly ever used.

The last of the coal trade to Leek ended in 1934 and, in 1939, the once active tar business between Leek and Milton also stopped. In 1944 the Leek branch was officially abandoned as it was deemed 'unnecessary'. After the Second World War, most of the other traffic subsided and in 1951, when the shipment of coal from Park Lane to Brittain's Paper Mills at Cheddleton stopped, the canal had no commercial traffic at all.

Following nationalization on 1 January 1948, boats continued to use the section to Hazlehurst, although the lines to Froghall and Leek were unnavigable. The canal was dredged in 1955 in an attempt to restart commercial coal-carrying to Froghall. When this failed, the future of the line looked bleak and a closure notice was duly posted at Etruria.

The Caldon Canal seemed doomed in 1961 but, in July, it was visited by the Inland Waterways Redevelopment Committee, a body set up to advise the Minister of Transport on disused canals. The scene of dereliction on the Caldon must have presented a challenge to the committee members who tried to walk along the overgrown towpath. Fortunately they recognized that the canal was fulfilling a vital function in supplying the T & M with water from its three active reservoirs and felt that it would be better if the line could be restored for navigation. A group of devotees met in 1963 and formed a committee to work for the restoration of the Caldon Canal. They brought together interested bodies, including the Staffordshire County Council and the Stoke-on-Trent City Council, and, on 4 April 1963, the Caldon Canal Committee became the Caldon Canal Society.

The rate of progress of restoration was inevitably slow, a situation that wasn't helped when the line was categorized as 'remainder' and not 'cruiseway' in the Transport Act of 1968. This categorisation gave the canal no permanent status in the eyes of the government and once again the entire future of the line depended on its role as a feeder for the T & M. But, through the actions of the Caldon Canal Society, on 22 August 1972 a two-year restoration programme was instigated when a new gate was installed at Engine Lock. This was followed by substantial renovation and dredging efforts from British Waterways. Cheddleton Top Lock and Waterworks Lock (at Stockton Brook) were completely rebuilt and major repairs were carried out to many of the other fourteen. A piped section near Froghall, that had been built in the early 1960s after some major landslips, was reopened for navigation as a concrete-lined channel.

All these efforts were rewarded on 28 September 1974 when the canal (including the Leek branch) was reopened for navigation as far as Froghall. The opening ceremony was performed at Cheddleton Top Lock. In 1983, the line was upgraded to cruiseway status and is today a highly popular and relaxing boating route.

Sir Frank Price lowers the lock gate at Engine Lock to mark the start of the restoration work on the Caldon Canal in 1972. The canal was fully restored and reopened on 28 September 1974

British Waterways

The Walk

Start:	Leek (OS ref: SJ 986564)
Finish:	Cheddleton (OS ref: SJ 973526)
Distance:	6¼ miles/10 km
Maps:	OS Landranger 118 (Stoke-on-Trent & Macclesfield) and 119 (Buxton, Matlock & Dovedale)
Return:	PMT buses run frequently between Cheddleton and Leek but there is only one service on Sundays (No. 76). Telephone: (0782) 223344
Car park:	Several signposted in town centre
Public transport:	PMT buses to Leek from Stoke which is itself on the BR main line. Telephone: (0782) 223344

From the centre of Leek, take the Stoke road (A53) for about a ¼ mile to the Safeways superstore (situated on the site of the old railway station) and The

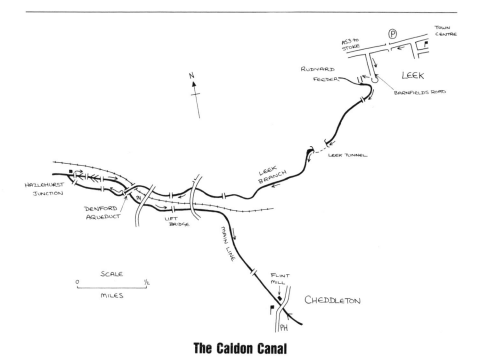

The Caldon Canal

Churnet Valley pub. Just after the pub is the site of the former Leek Wharf which, following the closure of the Leek branch of the canal, was purchased by the Leek Urban District Council in 1957 and converted into a trading estate. To reach the canal, turn left into Barnfields Road. Walk to the end of the road (not as far as it seems) to turn right along a narrow passageway between a wooden and a wire fence.

The path soon reaches a bridge that was in fact once the aqueduct which carried the line over the River Churnet and into Leek. Coming in from the right is what appears to be a small stream but is in fact the artificial feeder coming from the Rudyard reservoir some 3 miles to the north. The reservoir was an important source of water for the Trent & Mersey Canal and one of the major reasons for the construction of the Leek branch. It is said that Mr and Mrs Kipling named their son after a visit to the reservoir.

Turn left to follow the towpath around a bend to a winding hole (a last opportunity for boats to turn round) and a fine sandstone bridge (West Bridge). Already the scenery has forgotten the grubby trading estate and there are splendid views to the left and fields full of sheep to the right. The path follows a course around the contours to reach Leek Tunnel, 130 yd through solid sandstone. As there is no towpath through the tunnel, the path goes up over the hill. The effort involved is rewarded with a good view down to a small lagoon on the other side and over to a tall Gothic tower on the hill to the left, part of a hospital.

Continue down to the canal, which immediately bends left to go along a broad grassy track through a wooded stretch with mature trees and sandstone outcrops on the right-hand bank and fine views to the left. About a $\frac{3}{4}$ mile after the tunnel, the path goes under Waterworks Bridge and over a small wooden bridge which crosses a weir. In drier times the bridge doubles as a pleasant seat. A feeder on the far side of the weir appears miraculously to produce water from nowhere.

The canal now bends right with the Churnet Valley far down to the left. The view includes a railway line (now freight only) and, on the far hill, the Caldon Canal main line on its way to Cheddleton. Just before the next bridge (Horse Bridge), there is a stand full of stop planks: lengths of wood which slide down a groove cut into the sides of the canal to form a kind of temporary dam. Stop planks are used to isolate a stretch of the canal when there has either been a breach in the banks or when some maintenance is needed on the canal bed. The grooves for this set of planks can be seen just on the other side of the bridge.

The canal now bends left with a winding hole to the right. On the left is a splendid weir 'shoot' taking overflow water dramatically down to the River Churnet. The canal now winds past a pleasant group of houses and under two bridges to pass a British Waterways' yard. There are now two aqueducts in quick succession. The first, an innocuous affair which announces itself with a narrowing of the channel, passes over the railway line. There is then a short stretch before the second, and finer, structure – the Denford or Hazlehurst Aqueduct. This offers the fascinating sight of a canal over canal 'flyover', as the Leek branch goes over the Cheddleton main line. Here is the first part of the Hazlehurst Junction.

The Leek branch, and hence this junction, was added eighteen years after the main line to Froghall was built and it necessitated a major revision of this part of the canal. The original line, as it existed in 1797, had a $1\frac{1}{2}$ mile top pound between Stockton Brook Locks and Park Lane (about a mile and a half west from here). It then fell by three locks to Cheddleton. This original route can still be seen today because it roughly follows the course now taken by the railway. To accommodate the branch and, more importantly, the feeder water from the Rudyard reservoir, the company had to extend the summit pound and move the locks closer to Cheddleton so that the water was fed into the top level. This was done by building a new, higher cut to the south of the old line thereby allowing the summit pound to stretch all the way from Stockton to here at Denford. The Leek branch joined the main line at a point just on the Stockton side of a staircase of three locks. That point is just here where the canal turns abruptly right immediately after Denford Aqueduct. At that time, this stretch with the two aqueducts was simply an embankment which took the Leek branch across the valley to join with the main line. To go to Cheddleton or Froghall, boats turned left at this point to go through the staircase of three locks and down to the lower canal level.

This arrangement proved to be unsatisfactory, presumably because the staircase was causing too many delays. So, in 1841, the present design was devised. Part of the old line was reopened by cutting through the embankment to form the Denford Aqueduct. This new cut then continued to join the Leek branch at Hazlehurst Junction. The staircase locks were closed and that cut filled in. Three new locks were then built along the reopened stretch. What was a junction became a sudden right turn and what was an embankment became an aqueduct.

It is possible to go down the steps alongside the aqueduct to join the main line directly. However, it is more enjoyable to cross the canal at the footbridge and to continue along the Leek branch with the towpath now on the right-hand bank. There are good views of the main line, with its three locks, to the right. The canal bends round left to go under a bridge and then back right to another. Here is Hazlehurst Junction with its lock-keeper's cottage and fine cast-iron footbridge. The line goes on for a further $9\frac{1}{2}$ miles to Etruria where the canal has its junction with the Trent & Mersey. Our walk, however, turns nearly 180° right to pass the first Hazlehurst Lock (lock 10) with its cantilever bridge. The next two locks follow in quick succession, lock 11 having a neat brick-built hut.

To the left is the railway line which follows the original course of the canal

The first of the Hazlehurst Locks on the Caldon Canal

before the Leek branch was added. The point where the new route deviates can be seen where the canal bends suddenly right to pass under Denford (Hazlehurst) Aqueduct, a pleasant, unpretentious structure. Shortly after, the canal again bends suddenly, this time to the left. In the 1797 layout, the staircase locks were situated here to the right. We, meanwhile, are finally on the original course and pass the Hollybush at Denford pub.

The canal now borders the Deep Hayes Country Park to the right and passes under a bridge and then alongside Denford Lift Bridge. To the left, the Leek branch can be seen up on the side of the hill. After a fairly new road bridge (Wall Grange Bridge) and an old railway branch, a milepost reminds us that the canal once went to Uttoxeter. The towpath now passes over a wooden footbridge across a weir, similar to the one met on the Leek branch, and then proceeds gently to Cheddleton Wharf.

Here on the left is the site of the Cheddleton flint-grinding mill. Powdered flint was once used to whiten pottery. The first stage of the process involves 'calcining', a process in which the flints are heated to make them more brittle. With splendid efficiency, the kilns to do this have been built as part of the wharf. The flints were unloaded from the canal (the crane is still in position) into the tops of the kilns and then removed, after heating, at the bottom. The mills were operational by 1815 although there is evidence that the process was established here before then. Following their demise, the mills were restored by the Cheddleton Flint Mill Preservation Trust in the 1960s. It is said that James Brindley, who started as a millwright, may well have designed parts of these mills which are powered by undershot wheels. There is a small display here and the mill is open at weekends.

The towpath continues around some buildings to Cheddleton Bridge and a main road. Just the other side of the bridge are the two Cheddleton Locks which continue the descent of the canal to Froghall. At Cheddleton Top Lock, there is a plaque which commemorates the reopening of the canal in 1974.

Cheddleton has a small shop, a post office and some pubs: Old Flintlock, The Red Lion and The Black Lion. Buses for the return journey to Leek leave from the bus stop to the right on the mill side of the road.

Further Explorations

The entire length of the Caldon Canal is open to walkers: 17½ miles from Etruria to Froghall plus 3¾ miles from Hazlehurst to Leek.

A fine walk can be taken from Cheddleton to the end of the line at Froghall (OS Landranger map 119, ref: SK 027477): a distance of 6 miles. The only problem is that there is no ready transport between the two villages. However,

A typical Trent & Mersey Canal Company milepost on the Caldon Canal near Cheddington (note that this one was actually erected by the canal society in 1981)

those willing to walk both ways, or who have access to two cars, can enjoy some superb scenery. Cars can be parked at the picnic site at Froghall Wharf, a spot which is worth visiting even if you don't intend to walk anywhere. There are some fascinating old limekilns, the point where the Uttoxeter Canal formerly connected, a tunnel and, on summer Sunday afternoons, a horse-drawn boat which rides up and down the canal. The kilns obtained their supply of limestone via a horse tramroad and inclined plane from Caldon Low quarries 3 miles away. The course of the tramway runs straight on from the canal, running to the right if looking from the lime kilns. Lime burning continued here into the 1930s, although by then the limestone was transported down from Caldon Low by lorry.

The Uttoxeter Canal was opened in 1811 and closed in 1847. It ran for $13\frac{1}{2}$ miles. If you wish to trace it from Froghall, go from the wharf car park across the small road to the Caldon. A clear expansion of the waterway on the left-hand bank marks where the line started. Although long, long gone, it is still possible with the aid of an OS map to follow the course of the canal: through Oakamoor, past Alton Towers, through Denstone and into Uttoxeter.

It is $12\frac{1}{4}$ miles from Etruria to Leek and return journeys courtesy of PMT buses (albeit from Stoke) are frequent. From Etruria Junction (OS Land-ranger map 118, ref: SJ 872469), the route twists and turns through the outskirts of Hanley (with its numerous bottle kilns) and Hanley Park. The line soon fights its way to Foxley where the boats have to go through a kind of canal chicane before heading off towards Stockton Brook with its five locks. After Endon, you reach Hazlehurst Junction where you should take the right-hand course over the aqueduct for Leek.

At the Leek end of the canal, there is a popular walk of 3 miles each way along the feeder up to Rudyard reservoir. To reach the feeder follow the initial instructions for the main Leek to Cheddleton walk. The lake is very pleasant and highly frequented by fishermen.

Further Information

Although normally considered to be a branch of the Trent & Mersey, the Caldon has its own society:

Caldon Canal Society,
c/o W.G. Myatt,
Long Barrow,
Butterton,
Newcastle,
Staffs,
ST5 4EB.

The history of the Caldon Canal can be found within the pages of:
Lindsay, Jean, *The Trent & Mersey Canal*. David & Charles, 1979.
Hadfield, Charles, *The Canals of the West Midlands*. David & Charles, 1969.

However, most readers will probably find all they need in:
Lead, P., *The Caldon Canal and Tramroads*. The Oakwood Press, 1990.

4
THE CROMFORD CANAL
Ambergate to Cromford

Introduction

The village of Cromford, situated on the edge of the Peak District National Park just south of Matlock, is primarily known for its association with Sir Richard Arkwright and the birth of the factory system. Arkwright, who had developed the first successful water-powered cotton spinning mill, built his factory in the village away from the machine breakers and in an area where water power was both abundant and accessible. His only problem was transportation into and out of what was, at the time, a highly remote part of the country. The only way available to him was a hard and costly packhorse or wagon journey from the Lancashire ports. It comes as no surprise therefore to find Arkwright as one of the key protagonists in the construction of a canal to link his growing industrial village with the outside world. Although the collieries and quarries of the area produced more cargo for the line and although the great man died before the canal was opened, Arkwright's name will always be associated with this fine waterway.

The Cromford Canal is now only partly in water and large stretches are barely detectable on the ground. In its operational days, it started at a junction with the Erewash Canal, a line that runs from the River Trent near Long Eaton, through Ilkeston to Langley Mill near Eastwood. From Langley Mill, the Cromford Canal runs up the valley to Ironville, from where the Pinxton branch, of just under $2\frac{1}{2}$ miles, once ran to the north. Here the main line turns west to enter Butterley Tunnel at Golden Valley. It re-emerges, 3,063 yd later, near Bullbridge, where the navigation once crossed both the River Amber and the railway line via an aqueduct. At Ambergate, the line follows Derwent Valley through Crich Chase and Whatstandwell to Lea Wood, where a short, private branch once ran to the north. The final $1\frac{1}{2}$ miles of the canal begin where the line passes over the Derwent on Wigwell Aqueduct before continuing on to Cromford Wharf.

The northern section of the Cromford passes through some fine countryside which would have made good walking territory even if the canal had never been built. If one adds some fascinating industrial archaeology (apart from the canal there is a steam pumping station, the Cromford & High Peak Railway and, of course, Arkwright's Mill), then this walk makes for a splendid afternoon out.

History

The Erewash Canal runs for $11\frac{3}{4}$ miles from the River Trent to Langley Mill on the border between Derbyshire and Nottinghamshire near Heanor. Authorized by an Act of Parliament on 30 April 1777, the line was open for navigation just two years later, engineered by John Varley and built by John and James Pinkerton. The Erewash Canal was largely sponsored by local colliery owners and the line was an instant hit, with Derbyshire coal being shipped from the collieries around Eastwood, Ilkeston and Langley Mill to the River Trent at Long Eaton. From there, coal was moved both along the Trent and along the Soar Navigation into Leicestershire.

The success of the line soon prompted landowners further up Erewash Valley to consider an extension of the waterway to Pinxton, where a number of potential seams were said to be unworked because of the lack of transport. There was also considerable interest from the owners of the iron furnaces at Butterfly and Somercotes, of the limestone quarries at Crich, of the lead-works at Alderwasley and from Sir Richard Arkwright who had built his revolutionary cotton mills at Cromford. After some initial considerations, including the input of Arkwright and a meeting in Matlock, a line running from Langley Mill to Cromford, with a branch to Pinxton Mill, was proposed and widely agreed. At a meeting in Alfreton in December 1788, William Jessop presented his plan for the Cromford Canal together with an estimated cost of £42,697. Interest was such that half the necessary sum was raised at the meeting with the other half coming during the following two weeks. Peculiarly, the Erewash Canal Company contested the Cromford Act of 31 July 1789. Its objection was not to the canal *per se* but concerned its claimed exclusive rights to the water supplies from the River Erewash.

The line authorized was just over $14\frac{1}{2}$ miles long and had fourteen locks; all of which were south of Butterley Tunnel. The Act enabled the company to raise capital of £46,000. With Arkwright as company chairman, William Jessop was appointed engineer and Benjamin Outram and Thomas Dadford his assistants. Thomas Kearsley of Tamworth and Thomas Roundford of Coleridge, Staffordshire, were given the contracts for the work.

Not long after the construction work had started, it was realized that the project was going to run over budget, a situation that was not helped when the contractors absconded forcing the engineers to take direct control. By September 1791, all the initial monies had been spent and additional funds were raised by calls and loans. The year 1791 was also marked by the decision to proceed with the Nottingham Canal which would run from the Cromford, at a point just above Langley Mill, through Nottingham to the Trent. The supply of water along the line was a particular concern to the Cromford Company. This problem was originally overcome for the Cromford itself when Jessop had decided to dig an especially deep summit pound to act as a kind of *in situ* reservoir for water coming from the Cromford sough. If the Nottingham Canal was to take additional water then the problem was sure to become more acute. As part of the agreement between the two companies the Cromford only guaranteed water to the Nottingham if that company built extra reservoir capacity for both.

In February 1792 the line below Butterfly Tunnel was opened for traffic and

Boatmen 'legging' their narrowboat through Butterley Tunnel in about 1895. All tunnels that lacked a towpath had to be passed in this way while the horse took a more scenic route over the hill. 'Legged boats' took nearly three hours to go through the 3,063 yd long tunnel; just over a ½ mile per hour

British Waterways

receiving tolls. However, the 200 yd long and 50 ft high Amber Aqueduct near Ambergate was already in need of partial rebuilding. Jessop, who appears to have had a reputation for indifferent masonry work, accepted responsibility for the faults and paid the £650 needed to undertake the repairs. The situation repeated itself in 1792 when Wigwell Aqueduct over the Derwent was closed for some time as it too needed partial rebuilding. Again Jessop accepted responsibility, admitting that the failure was due to the lack of strength in the front walls. With the aqueducts repaired and the rest of the line, including the tunnel, ready, the line was fully opened in August 1794. The final cost was £78,880: twice the estimate.

This gross over-expenditure was soon forgotten as the canal was an almost instant success. In 1802–3, the line carried over 150,000 tons of cargo, of which some 110,000 tons were coal and coke and nearly 30,000 tons lime and limestone. The stone for St George's Hall in Liverpool, for example, was carried along this route. In 1802, the privately owned Lea Wood branch was opened providing canal access to a number of works and quarries in the Lea Wood area (south-east of Cromford). At about the same time plans were produced for a similar branch to Bakewell, although this line was never built.

By 1814 the company was doing well enough to be able to pay a dividend of 10 per cent, a sum that reached 18 per cent in 1830 and 28 per cent in 1841. By that time traffic along the Cromford Canal as a whole had almost doubled from the 1802–3 levels to nearly 290,000 tons. Almost twice as much coal and coke was now being carried and there had been substantial increases in the carriage of farm produce and other quarried materials such as ironstone and gritstone. Iron from the Butterley works also increased considerably during this period. Much of the coal traffic passed down the Cromford Canal and along the Erewash to be taken onto the Soar Navigation for sale in the Leicester area. Interestingly, the dramatic increases in stone were partially the result of the increased demand for railway ballast. Charles Hadfield reported that large quantities of Cromford stone were used on the London & Birmingham Railway.

The canal was connected to the collieries and quarries by means of tramways varying in length from a $\frac{1}{4}$ to $1\frac{1}{2}$ miles. The Crich limestone quarries, for example, had a tramway outlet to the canal at Bullbridge. This line was later taken across the canal to meet with the Midland Railway. At Riddings, a donkey-drawn tramway was in operation, while at Birchwood and Swanwick, a steam-driven system was used. At Butterley, the ironworks, which were producing cannon and shot for the Woolwich Arsenal, were connected to the canal by means of two shafts down which cargo was lowered on to barges in the tunnel below.

In addition to the freight traffic, from September 1797, a packet boat for passengers, run by Nathaniel Wheatcroft of Cromford, operated twice weekly between Cromford Wharf and Nottingham, a distance of 38 miles. First class travellers paid 5s. for this trip while second class passengers paid just 3s.

By far the most important of the railway developments occurred between the canal at Lea Wood and the Peak Forest Canal at Whaley Bridge. The link was originally conceived as a canal navigation. Indeed, John Rennie had carried out a preliminary survey and presented an estimate of £650,000. The line was thought by many, including the highly supportive Grand Junction Canal Company (now known as the Grand Union), to be a way of shortening the route from London to Manchester. Naturally the Trent & Mersey, whose business was most under threat, was antagonistic and it appears to have won the argument. But the concept stayed alive and it was not long before thoughts had switched to a railway line, now known as the Cromford & High Peak. Following an Act of 2 May 1825, Josias Jessop, son of William, was appointed engineer and work began. The line, which opened on 6 July 1831, included stationary engines to haul wagons up as many as nine inclines to the more conventional railways that ran along the summit. One of the inclines can be seen clearly from the A6 just south of Cromford. The line was an important conduit for various cargoes going north–south, including agricultural produce and even water. The company faced severe competition by the late 1840s from other railway lines but the route remained open until 1967. It is now part of a long-distance path: the High Peak Trail.

In the 1830s, competition from the Staffordshire collieries led the Cromford company to halve its tolls for cargoes of Derbyshire coal destined for the Grand Junction Canal. However, as this action had no effect on the level of traffic, the concession was withdrawn. But, in the 1840s, the more direct competition of the new railways was beginning to be realised and toll reductions were made in order simply to compete. By 1843 the effects of doing this were already being felt: toll revenue had decreased by a quarter in just two years and the company was forced to halve its annual dividend.

There was also a growing problem with water supply during the 1840s. The original main source, the Cromford sough, which ran from local lead mines through Arkwright's Mill and into the canal at Cromford Wharf, was stopped when the mines were worked at a lower level. The company were forced to build a pumping station near Wigwell Aqueduct to lift water from the Derwent up to the canal summit level.

Although there appears to have been some thought to cooperation with its canal neighbours, the Cromford Canal Company saw the inevitability of the railway age fairly early – in fact some time before the main competitive line, the Erewash Valley line, was even finished. The company sought and reached agreement with the Manchester, Buxton, Matlock & Midlands Junction Railway, the company which planned to build the line from Cheadle to Ambergate. The MBM & MJR bought the Cromford for £103,500, a deal which has since been seen as excellent salesmanship by the Cromford board. The sale was completed, after the passage of an Act, on 30 August 1852. Shortly thereafter the MBM & MJR leased the line jointly to the Midland Railway and

The 200 yd long Bullbridge Aqueduct in 1900 carried the canal over the River Amber, the railway and the road near Ambergate. After the canal closed, the aqueduct was demolished to make way for a road-widening scheme

The Boat Museum archive

the London and North Western. By 1870 it was a wholly owned part of the Midland.

As soon as the canal entered into railway hands, the level of traffic along the line declined. With the Midland Railway running alongside the waterway for its entire length, the canal was never in a good position to compete. From traffic of 300,000 tons in 1849, only 145,814 tons were carried in 1870 and 45,799 in 1888. These figures also disguise the fact that traffic was becoming increasingly local, with long-distance transport being taken almost entirely by rail.

The end of the canal as a going concern began in 1889 when subsidence in Butterley Tunnel forced temporary closure and the expenditure of £7,364 on repairs. By May 1893, the line was reopened but the traffic through the tunnel was down to less than 4,000 tons p.a. On 5 July 1900, a second collapse in the tunnel led to its final closure and the route was cut in half permanently. In 1904, Rudolph de Salis reported that the headroom was very low and the brickwork lining the tunnel was in a very dangerous condition. The whole issue was sealed with a third collapse in February 1907. The stone traffic from Whatstandwell to the south was transferred to the railway at no extra cost to the shippers and, in 1909, a Royal Commission pronounced the tunnel beyond economic repair.

Below the tunnel, traffic remained reasonably vigorous with some 39,000 tons being moved in 1905. North of the tunnel, a small amount of traffic continued with coal being shipped into Cromford and lead being taken from Lea Wood along the private arm to High Peak Wharf where it was transhipped on to rail. With the closure of the Lea Wood arm in 1936, the London, Midland & Scottish Railway (which had become the owners after the great railway amalgamations of 1923) announced their intention to close the canal on 13 March 1937. Although there were some objections, with the canal at one stage being offered free to the Grand Union Canal Company, all but the southernmost ½ mile was officially abandoned in 1944. The last ½ mile was finally closed in 1962.

Although the southern section of the Cromford has mostly disappeared into the undergrowth, in 1974 the Derbyshire County Council bought the northernmost 5½ miles from Ambergate to Cromford for use as a public amenity. With the assistance of various voluntary groups, the last 1½ miles of the canal has been made into a popular linear country park and is used extensively by towpath walkers and holiday makers.

The Walk

Start:	Ambergate station (OS ref: SK 348516)
Finish:	Cromford (OS ref: SK 299571)
Distance:	5½ miles/8½ km
Map:	OS Outdoor Leisure 24 (The White Peak)
Return:	Train Cromford to Ambergate. Also runs on Sundays. Telephone: (0332) 32051
Car parks:	At picnic site at Cromford end of canal (signposted from A6), at Ambergate station or at Whatstandwell station
Public transport:	BR to stations on Derby–Matlock line

As some of the most interesting features of the canal are towards the northern (Cromford) end of the line, this walk can be conveniently shortened to 3 miles by walking to Cromford from Whatstandwell station (OS ref: SK 333541).

For the full walk, leave Ambergate station car park to return to the main road (the A610 to Nottingham) and turn left to go under the railway bridge. Turn right along the A6 to pass the Little Chef roadside restaurant. After about 250 yd, turn right along Chase Road, following a footpath sign that promises Bullbridge and Fritchley. Go under the railway to a small bridge over the canal. Turn left to go along the towpath which is on the left-hand bank.

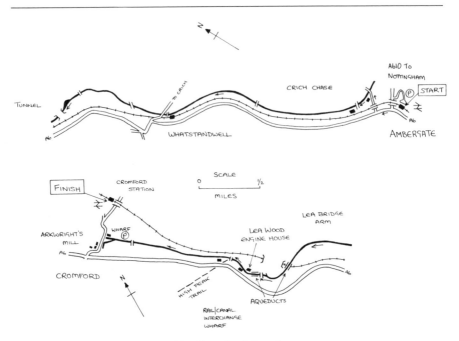

The Cromford Canal

The canal here is very overgrown with weeds suggesting that we have yet to reach the manicured, tourist section which is within easy reach of Cromford. The line soon goes under a bridge and we pass the first of several lengthman's cottages to be seen along the waterway. The job of lengthman must appear idyllic to many modern-day canal enthusiasts who have donned rose-tinted spectacles. The lengthman walked his allocated stretch of the line daily: opening sluice gates to release excess water, unblocking weirs, keeping a wary eye for potential breaches, maintaining the towpath, inspecting the culverts, bridges and tunnels. Keeping the water level up and ensuring that all the feeder channels were clear and operational were the particular concerns in summer. The lengthman would also have looked after the canal's boundaries and maintained the hedges and ditches. It was a poorly paid job and, without doubt, much tougher than our romantic back-glances might suggest. It must be said, however, that if you were going to be one then this was as good a place as any.

The canal is now on the side of a hill with both the railway and the road down the slope to the left. The right-hand side, meanwhile, is lined with a dense stand of alder trees. Just before the second cottage (used by the local St John's Ambulance group) is a small milepost announcing that we are still 4½ miles from Cromford Wharf. The woodland that now lines both sides of the canal is known as Crich Chase. In the early nineteenth century, the concern over poaching was such that a by-law was introduced which prohibited boatmen from mooring here overnight.

The way winds quietly and pleasantly onwards to Whatstandwell. Those joining the route here should leave the station and turn right to reach the Derwent Hotel. Turn right along a road signposted to Crich and the Tramway Museum. Within 100 yd, the road crosses the canal. Turn left to join the walk.

The canal runs along the base of a steep hill on top of which once stood Duke's quarries. At one point, the abutments of a tramway bridge, coming down from the Crich limestone quarries, still stand but now bear nothing but the weight of a small footbridge. The canal just here is stone-lined and is bordered by stop plank grooves, both suggestions of persistent breaches in the line. For a short distance the canal narrows so that the towpath appears wider than the waterway. It then passes a fine house before bending gradually to the left. The views to the left now show that the canal has retained the northern side of the valley whereas the river, railway and A6 have taken the southern side. Shortly, the canal goes under a bridge (with stop planks in position) and then broadens at Gregory Dam before entering a short tunnel with a convenient towpath that goes all the way through.

The line passes the Derwent Nature Reserve amid dense woodland before running around the contours of the hillside to reach an aqueduct which takes the canal over the railway. The Cromford now bends right around the hill to reach Lea Wood Junction. On the right is another derelict lengthman's cottage buried in the undergrowth and just beyond are the remains of the Lea Wood branch. This cut was built by Peter Nightingale, Florence's father, who shared the cost with the Cromford Canal Company. It was opened in early 1802 and ran just a $\frac{1}{2}$ mile to his own wharves at Lea Wood where there were two lead-works, cotton mills, a hat factory and a group of quarries. The Lea Wood cut was closed in March 1936 and is now dry. An iron aqueduct which carried the branch over the railway has sadly been removed.

Although it is possible to follow the Lea Wood branch, we stay on the main line. Cross the canal at the swing bridge and turn left to walk over Wigwell Aqueduct. Wigwell crosses the River Derwent on three arches, the centre one of which spans 80 ft. The aqueduct as a whole is 200 yd long and 30 ft high. Although it's solid enough now, it must have been a moving source of embarrassment to William Jessop. In September 1793, cracks appeared in the outer walls: a fault which Jessop blamed on the quality of the lime used in the mortar. Instead of setting, the cement stayed soft and allowed the masonry to bulge outwards. Jessop accepted responsibility for the fault and had the good grace to pay for the repairs out of his own pocket. The structure was made good by incorporating iron bars into the stonework in order to prevent the walls from crumbling. Given that Jessop was earning £350 p.a. as engineer and that he had already paid £650 for the repair work on Amber Aqueduct, his work on the Cromford can be seen to have been anything but a profitable exercise.

The Lea Wood pumping
station and Wigwell
Aqueduct

Continue along the path and up to the fine Lea Wood pumping house. The building was put up in 1849 to raise water from the River Derwent to the canal. This proved necessary when supplies of water from the Cromford sough feeder were restricted through changes in mining practice in Cromford. It is constructed of local gritstone. The chimney is some 95 ft high and has a rather curious splayed parapet which is made of cast iron. The building houses a Boulton & Watt type single-acting beam engine that was built by Graham & Co. The beam is nearly 33 ft long and the pump can raise between 20 and 30 tons of water per minute through a hidden tunnel system that passes underneath the building. The engine has been restored by the Cromford Canal Society and is periodically open to the public. At the time of writing, however, this situation is somewhat confused (see below).

The walk continues along the well-restored towpath to pass High Peak Wharf where a canal/railway interchange shed still stands with its awning overhanging the line. This was the terminus of the 33 mile long Cromford & High Peak Railway. From here the railway ran alongside the canal for a short distance before rising up an incline to a 12 mile long summit level at 1,271 ft. In the days of horse-drawn trains, the journey to the Peak Forest Canal at Whaley Bridge took over six hours. Although the prime traffic along the line was limestone, there was also a small number of passenger carriages. The line was opened fully on 6 July 1831 and closed as recently as 1967.

A little further on are various other buildings associated with the railway. The railway company had its workshops here including a servicing shed which has an inspection pit laid with original 4 ft fish-bellied rails lettered 'C & HP Railway'. There is also a charming (to look at rather than live in) row of railway workers' cottages.

If you cross the canal at the next swing bridge, you can visit High Peak Junction. The first inclined plane leads off from here and can be seen disappearing up the hill to the left. Originally this incline consisted of two separate planes with individual rises of 204 ft and 261 ft. They were combined in 1857 and were worked as one 1,320 yd long slope with a gradient of between 1:8 and 1:9. Until 1964, trucks were hauled up the hill by a steam engine that was housed in another fine engine house. This was replaced by an electric motor for the final three years of operation. The problem was that during the period when the new motor was installed, the prime user (Middleton Quarry) found the replacement road traffic simpler and cheaper to use. In working the system, trucks were attached to a wire rope to form trains in which ascending wagons were balanced by those descending. In the early days, runaway trucks hurtling uncontrollably downhill were a regular and highly dangerous problem. The situation was alleviated (if not cured) by the construction of special pits into which runaways were diverted so that they could smash themselves to pieces in relative safety.

At the junction there are a couple of restored trucks and, in the small workshop building, an information centre, a display of various artefacts, and a small shop. Around the corner are toilets and a picnic area.

Return across the swing bridge and turn left. It is now just a short walk, under a small accommodation bridge, to Cromford Wharf. This first announces itself on the canal line with a winding hole, where boats were able to turn, and to the right with a large, recently constructed, car park. On the top of the hill to the left is Sir Richard Arkwright's home which was appropriately called the Rock House. The archway near the winding hole is the boathouse for Rock House.

The entire area of the wharf was formerly Arkwright's garden and was bought from him by the canal company. It should be said that Arkwright himself had every intention of moving and was building himself a mansion just up the road. The wharf was opened in 1794 and, away from the canal to the right, there are various buildings which were originally (from right to left): a sawpit, a smithy, a

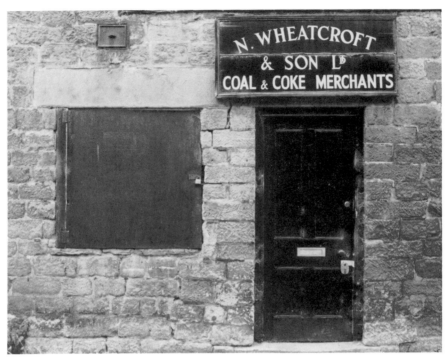

Nathaniel Wheatcroft's offices at Cromford Wharf

stable and some canal workers' cottages. The canal itself forks to two wharves which the canal company divided in function. The area opposite the winding hole was reserved for incoming coal shipments. The right-hand fork of the canal was used for incoming timber and other goods while the left-hand fork was used for outgoing cargo such as limestone and lead. The first canalside buildings were those on the far left-hand side: a warehouse and, beyond, a counting house or company office. These were both built in 1794. The warehouse with the covered area on the right was built in 1824 by Nathaniel Wheatcroft who at the time was a major canal carrier. The Wheatcroft family also acted as wharfingers and were at one time coal merchants. In the 1830s, German Wheatcroft & Sons operated passenger services to various parts of the country, including London and Bristol, three days a week. German also operated a passenger 'fly' up and down the Cromford & High Peak Railway. Nathaniel Wheatcroft operated services to Nottingham and the Potteries on Tuesdays and Fridays.

Continue past the right-hand warehouse and turn left to walk around the back of the wharf. Here it can be seen that the left-hand fork of the canal extends to the road from where it narrows considerably to bend left around the rocky outcrop that forms the foundations of Rock House. This is the feeder channel that carries water from Cromford sough via Arkwright's Mills which stand beyond.

Arkwright's Mills have now been taken over by the Arkwright Society whose intention is to restore the main part of the building to its original working state while letting the rest as office space for small companies. The mills are open to visitors and there is a small gift shop and café on site.

To return to Ambergate, turn right when leaving the wharf area to pass St Mary's parish church. This leads to a bridge which crosses the Derwent. Continue along the right-hand road to a point where a sign points left to Cromford station. This fine, sadly neglected station offers regular trains to Whatstandwell and Ambergate, even on Sundays!

Further Explorations

There's not a lot of Cromford Canal left to explore but it is worth having a quick look at Butterley Tunnel. The eastern portal can be reached from Golden Valley (OS Landranger map 120, ref: SK 423512). This point is on the Newlands Road between Codnor and Somercotes. At the Newlands Inn, take a path that goes down the left-hand side to reach the very overgrown canal. This area has been converted into a nature reserve and walk. After about 200 yd, the path rises slightly and those with penetrative sight should be able to make out the barred portal of the tunnel over to the right.

The tunnel is 3,063 yd long and was built narrow, in other words unsuitable for barges. The locks to the south were all wide enough to allow Erewash barges to serve the collieries up to the tunnel but not beyond. As there was no room for two boats to pass each other mid-tunnel, traffic through it was carefully regulated. Westward boats were allowed entry between 5 and 6 a.m. and 1 and 2 p.m., and those going east between 9 and 10 a.m. and 5 and 6 p.m. In 1802, when traffic had increased, the tunnel was worked at night and additional entry times were allowed at the east end between 9 and 10 p.m. and the west from 1 and 2 a.m. Three hours were allowed for passage which may seem a little excessive but was due to the fact that this was a 'legging' tunnel. Here men known as 'leggers' lay on their sides on the boat and literally walked their way through with their feet pressing against the walls.

The channel that comes in from the right of the tunnel is a feeder from Butterley reservoir. The stepped weir down to the canal is typical of situations where the supply reservoir was built at a level considerably above that of the waterway.

After returning to the Newlands Inn and crossing the road, a public footpath follows the course of the canal to Ironville and beyond. It is possible to follow paths to Langley Mill although the canal disappears long before reaching the Erewash.

Further Information

The Cromford Canal Society is not at present operational. Hopefully a restructured group will emerge to safeguard the interests of this wonderful waterway and, perhaps, even strive to rejoin it to the Erewash.

The history of the Cromford Canal, together with the Erewash and the Nottingham, is described in:
Hadfield, Charles, *The Canals of the East Midlands*. David & Charles, 1966.

A shortened history of the Cromford and other canals in Derbyshire can be found in:
Smith, M., *Derbyshire Canals*. J.H. Hall & Sons Ltd, 1987.

The Arkwright Society published a local history trail leaflet on the canal. This is available at the Arkwright Mill in Cromford.

Those tempted by the High Peak Trail along the Cromford & High Peak Railway should refer to a cousin of this volume:
Vinter, J., *Railway Walks: LMS*. Alan Sutton Publishing, 1990.

5
THE GRANTHAM CANAL
Bottesford to Grantham

Introduction

Grantham is now more popularly famous for its grocer's daughter than for its commercial activity but it was once an important market town for the rich farmlands of Lincolnshire. Its importance was heightened when the local entrepreneurs sponsored the construction of a canal for the import and export of coal and agricultural produce. Although the new waterway forged a tangible link with the industry and collieries around the city of Nottingham, the Lincolnshire countryside remained remote from industrial development, as it does to this day. The canal, now long-closed and virtually boat-free, retains a feeling of loneliness and isolation, which it probably always will, despite being subject to an enthusiastic restoration programme.

The 33 mile long Grantham Canal leaves the River Trent at West Bridgford within sight of Trent Bridge and the Nottingham Forest football ground. After going through the now closed Trent Lock, the canal soon becomes impassable as various new bridges and embankments block the original line effectively to seal this route forever. The situation remedies itself as the canal winds south and then east to pass to the north of Nottingham airport. Here the waterway is carried over Pulser Brook on a small aqueduct. If restoration plans are enacted, the canal will use the northerly course of this brook to take it to a new junction with the Trent at the Holme Pierrepoint water sports centre.

After passing to the north of the colliery village of Cotgrave, the line turns south to go past Cropwell Bishop to Hickling. Here the canal reverts to a north-easterly course as it meanders through the Vale of Belvoir to Redmile. Broad zigzags now take the canal near Bottesford and Woolsthorpe before passing Denton reservoir to come to an end at the A1 embankment. On the other side there remains just a short stretch to Earles Field Bridge beyond which the original line into Grantham Basin has been filled in and, perhaps appropriately given the location, privatized.

The Grantham has no dramatic scenery or startling architectural structures but it does offer a pleasant, peaceful walk through the arable countryside that typifies the Vale of Belvoir. It also has the additional interest of a canal in restoration, the seemingly impossible challenge that tests the ingenuity and tenacity of the most devout of enthusiasts. Walk it before it becomes popular.

History

The last decade of the eighteenth century, the period often referred to as the time of canal mania, saw considerable waterway construction and improvement both in and around the city of Nottingham. Most of this activity concerned the building of canals to take the products of collieries and quarries on to an ever more navigable River Trent and from there to markets in the south. Although it had no quarries the small town of Grantham, some 21 miles to the east of Nottingham, clearly wanted to be involved. The businessmen of Grantham, who were obliged to pay high rates for land transport of their goods to Newark-on-Trent or to the port of Boston, liked the idea of a canal to connect the town with the ever expanding waterway network. The appeal was in the potential for cheap carriage of their own goods and in the access to a plentiful and cheap supply of coal from the Derbyshire fields.

William Jessop, who had been busy in the area surveying the Nottingham Canal, was approached by the Grantham businessmen and asked to make a survey of a line from the Trent to Grantham. In a plan that was announced on 27 August 1791, Jessop proposed a contour canal leaving the River Trent at Radcliffe, a point to the east of Nottingham city centre. The enthusiasm generated for the line was such that all £40,000 of the estimated cost was raised at this single meeting. A bill based on Jessop's plan was presented to Parliament in 1792 but was rejected due to objections from local landowners and from those who feared loss of overland trade to Newark. Waterway-related opposition was also evident from those with interests in the prospective Grantham to Newark canal and from those who feared that the River Witham would lose water.

Jessop re-surveyed the junction with the Trent and devised a new line to West Bridgford, just 1 mile from the modern Nottingham city centre. There was also to be a 3½ mile long branch to Bingham, a village about 8 miles due east of Nottingham. With less opposition, this Act was more successful and was passed on 30 April 1793. Capital of £75,000 was authorized with £30,000 in reserve if required. On top of the specified toll rates, an additional charge of 2½d. per ton was permitted for all cargo entering or leaving the River Trent. The proprietors of the Trent Navigation were obliged by the Act to keep the Trent Lock entrance dredged to a minimum of 3 ft in order to guarantee access to the new line.

By 1910, hardly any cargo traffic used the canal and so pleasure boating and fishing became popular, as here at Earle's Field Bridge in Grantham

The Boat Museum archive

The canal was to be one of 33 miles, not including the branch to Bingham which seems to have been quietly dropped. Jessop's rather old fashioned contour canal meandered through the Vale of Belvoir passing small villages and gradually rising by about 140 ft to reach Grantham town centre. Although Grantham businessmen occupied most of the seats on the board, the principal shareholders were from Nottingham. Two engineers were appointed to build the line. James Green was asked to take charge of the line from the Trent to the Leicestershire boundary near Hickling. Green was employed by Lord Middleton at Wollaton Hall and came with the approval of Jessop with whom he had worked on the Nottingham Canal. For the rest of the line into Grantham, the board appointed William King, agent to the Duke of Rutland at Belvoir. The Duke owned that stretch and clearly must have had a say in his appointment. King was also made responsible for the construction of the two main reservoirs: the Denton and the Knipton, the latter of which was formed after damming the River Devon. Jessop was called in as consultant, presumably to keep a check on the otherwise comparatively inexperienced engineers.

By February 1797, King's eastern end was reported to be navigable and the first traffic probably passed along the route during the following April. There was some minor delay at the western end, caused by problems with the gypsum under rock near Cropwell Bishop. Despite this, the whole line was opened for traffic during the course of the summer. The main engineering feature was the long cutting through Harlaxton Drift, near Grantham. This was originally only able to take narrowboats and had two passing places so that traffic wasn't overly inconvenienced. The line here was widened later. The completed canal had cost £118,500, the extra funds having been raised by additional calls on shares and by obtaining loans. The line had eighteen broad locks able to take craft measuring 75 ft by 14 ft. The only tricky portion of the line was at the Trent entrance where to get into the Trent Lock (No. 1) a rope and capstan had to be used to haul boats round.

Almost immediately the canal company started its own trade in coal and coke. Others started shipping lime, building materials and groceries from Nottingham and various types of agricultural produce (corn, malt, beans and wool) back into town. Before too long Grantham was to become a port for the wide area of rich, Lincolnshire farmlands that surround it. By 1798, the canal was also carrying people, a passenger boat having been introduced between Nottingham and Cotgrave on Saturdays

In 1803, the company was able to pay its first dividend, albeit only of 2 per cent. But by 1815 a sizeable proportion of the debts had been repaid and the dividend had risen to 5 per cent with total toll revenue never exceeding £9,000 p.a. Traffic continued to grow and reached a peak in 1841 with toll receipts of £13,079. To maintain this relatively high revenue level the company kept its toll charges up despite the protestations of the canal users. At one stage the company was accused of maintaining too high a toll for coal traffic and was indicted for conspiracy to enhance prices. Such overcharging appears to have had the affect of making some traders seek alternative routes into and out of Grantham. One trader, for example, found it cheaper to import coal overland from Newark than along the canal. The Oakham and Melton Mowbray Navigations were also able, by reducing their own tolls, to capture a lot of the grain traffic from the Grantham line. Despite the accusations and the loss of traffic to competitors, the canal maintained its pricing policy and appears to have remained moderately successful.

This situation continued until 1845 when the company found itself confronted with railway competition and decided (along with the Nottingham Canal) that its best interest was to sell out to the potential rival, namely the Nottingham, Vale of Belvoir & Grantham Railway. This it duly did on the proviso that the railway company built and opened its Ambergate–Grantham line. Before the railway had got around to this, however, it had undergone a merger to become the Ambergate, Nottingham, Boston & Eastern Junction Railway.

The rail line from Nottingham to Grantham was opened on 15 July 1850, the rest being left for a more favourable economic climate. However, the planned take-over was held up by the railway company's unwillingness to part with any funds. The problem was partly related to a cash-flow problem and partly because the ANB & EJR had plans to link with the Great Northern Railway (which owned and operated the main line from London to Grantham). The GNR was known to be unwilling to waste funds on money-losing canals and the ANB & EJR must have been eager to show that it was of similar mind. The Grantham and Nottingham Canal Companies were thus forced to take legal action in order to compel the railway company to honour its agreement and pay up. This it eventually did on 20 December 1854. The company now became the Ambergate, Nottingham, Boston & Eastern Junction Railway and Canal Company. Three months later the ANB & EJR & C Co. obtained its longed for agreement with the Great Northern Railway Company who would now work the Grantham to Nottingham line. Having giving up all pretence of ever reaching Ambergate the company changed its name in 1860 to the Nottingham and Grantham Railway and Canal Company and a year later leased itself to the GNR for a period of 999 years.

The GNR now had canals that it didn't want and, indeed, canals that were in open competition with its own railway. As a result the GNR did little to promote or develop the canal and trade steadily declined. Despite this, some 18,802 tons

The Cameron sisters took advantage of the traffic-free canal by hiring out pleasure boats from Grantham Basin. This picture was taken in the 1920s. The warehouses in the background were demolished in October 1929

G. Knapp, The Boat Museum archive

of cargo were recorded in 1905, comprising mostly of manure and roadstone, yielding tolls of just £242. By 1924 (by which time the canal had become just a minute part of the massive London and North Eastern Railway) this had reduced to 1,583 tons and most of the regular traffic had long gone. By 1929, trade had stopped almost completely and the line was legally abandoned in 1936 under the London & North Eastern Railway (General Powers) Act. The LNER argued that many of the lock gates needed replacing and that the expense of undertaking the work simply wasn't warranted.

Fortunately for us, the canal has remained mostly in water as it is used as a kind of linear reservoir. The various canal structures have usually only been demolished when they have fallen down, become subject to vandalism, or where road-works have enforced bridge strengthening or road widening. Unfortunately this latter activity has led to two major obstacles: a series of blockages in West Bridgford and the A1 dual carriageway near Grantham. These two sets of road-works have effectively sealed both ends of the canal. In addition all of the locks, other than Trent Lock, have been de-gated and converted into weirs.

In 1969, the Grantham Canal Society, now called the Grantham Canal Restoration Society Ltd, was formed with the aim of restoring the waterway to cruising standards and reconnecting it to the rest of the canal network. This noble intention will need some major works at the two sealed ends. At the Nottingham end, current plans are to build a wholly new line to the Trent. This would take the canal north after Lock 4 to join Pulser Brook as it passes under the A52 to Holme Pierrepoint. In among the gravel diggings in the area, a 2000 m rowing course has been dug and the new canal junction and marina are being considered at SK 396630. The A1 may be even more of a problem as digging a fresh tunnel through the road embankment would be prohibitively expensive. However, where there's life . . .

The Walk

Start:	Bottesford station (OS ref: SK 810393)
Finish:	Grantham Old Wharf (OS ref: SK 905350)
Distance:	10½ miles/17 km
Map:	OS Landranger 130 (Grantham)
Outward:	Train Grantham to Bottesford. Also runs on Sundays Telephone: (0476) 64135
Car park:	Grantham railway station
Public transport:	BR Nottingham to Grantham line

Grantham has a busy railway station for such a small town, mostly as a result of

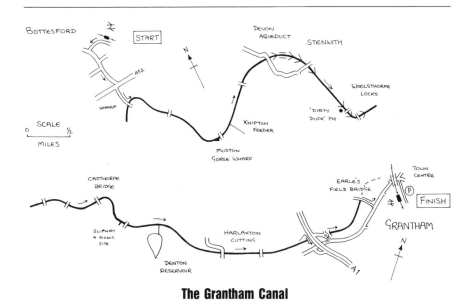

The Grantham Canal

the fact that it is on the main line from London to York and Scotland. The line from Grantham to Bottesford is a side issue in comparison but can be used for the outward journey having parked the car in the station car park.

From Bottesford station turn right to follow the road around left with the church to the left. Turn left at Rectory Lane (a T-junction) following signs for Belvoir. This leads to Grantham Road. Pass the Bull Inn and then bear left along Belvoir Road. This passes some houses to reach the A52 Grantham to Nottingham road (Bottesford bypass). Cross this busy road and follow signs to Belvoir Castle. As this minor road bends left and rises towpathers will sigh with relief as they reach Bottesford Bridge and the Grantham Canal.

Before starting on the walk, go up to the bridge and look down right. Here, as the towpath widens to bend under the bridge, is the site of the former Bottesford Wharf. To start the walk turn down left to take the towpath which is on the left-hand bank. Immediately to the left is a small notice board describing the route taken by the canal together with a milepost which indicates $24\frac{1}{4}$ miles from the River Trent at West Bridgford. Further notices and mileposts occur at regular intervals between here and Grantham.

The canal shortly enters a cutting through Toston Hill around which the sounds of the kennels to the right echo ominously. The cutting soon shallows and, a $\frac{1}{4}$ mile further on, the canal reaches the culverted Easthorpe or Middlestile Bridge. A number of the bridges along the route have become culverts since the canal was officially abandoned in 1936. To reopen the line each bridge will have to be raised with all the consequent roadworks involved in building the embankments required on both sides of the road.

Muston Gorse Wharf with Belvoir Castle in the distance

The canal now passes through open country with Belvoir Castle visible over to the right. After the canal has gone through a double bend, it widens on the right-hand bank to form Muston Gorse Wharf. From here a private tramway, owned by the Duke of Rutland, formerly took coal and other goods up to the castle which is approximately $1\frac{1}{2}$ miles away.

The canal continues past Muston Gorse Bridge. A little way further on, the feeder channel from the Knipton reservoir enters the canal. The reservoir is some 3 miles to the south near the village of Knipton. Chris Cove-Smith points out that for 1 mile of its journey it is carried through a tunnel under Belvoir Castle. The canal, meanwhile, continues on for a $\frac{1}{2}$ mile to Langore Bridge, an original accommodation type bridge built to permit the local farmer to pass from one side of the canal to the other. The sides of the bridge still bear the marks of the many towropes that have passed this way. A $\frac{1}{4}$ mile further on, the canal leaves Nottinghamshire to enter Lincolnshire near a winding hole or turning point. The line then reaches the relatively new Muston Bridge followed by the first of the Woolsthorpe flight of locks: Woolsthorpe Bottom or Muston Lock. All the locks along this stretch of the canal have been de-gated and converted into weirs. Their renovation is one of the first priorities of the Grantham Canal Restoration Society. The dilapidated state of some of the locks, however, means they will need complete rebuilding – a difficult job when virtually all the labour to be used will be volunteers who will only be able to work at weekends or during summer camps.

To the left from here until we reach the outskirts of Woolsthorpe the left-hand side of the canal is occupied by the line of the former ironstone railway which joins the course of the canal from Belvoir Junction on the main line near Bottesford. This line was built by the Great Northern Railway after they had taken control of the canal in 1861. The line (known as the Belvoir branch) was opened in 1883 much to the annoyance of the local boatmen and the canal carriers who had been confidently predicting an increase in canal traffic when the Stanton Ironworks Company started their excavations for iron ore at Brewers Grave (a ½ mile east of Woolsthorpe) in 1879. Traffic along the line appears to have stopped as recently as 1973. The course of the tramway can still be seen as a clear track between two rows of trees and bushes on the other side of the fence to the left. At one point, just before the next lock, the trestles are all that remain of an old railway bridge across the tiny River Devon. This also marks the position of a small aqueduct which carries the canal over the same river.

The next lock is Stenwith Lock and it has an associated keeper's cottage, now a private house. After the crumbling Kingston's Lock, towpathers go under Stenwith Bridge to reach Woolsthorpe Middle Lock. This heralds the start of a ½ mile straight section known as Half Mile Pond. This ends at Carpenter's Lock and Woolsthorpe Bridge where the Rutland Arms (locally known as the Dirty Duck) offers sustenance. Those who are tempted may wish to know that there are about 5 miles to go to Grantham. Just after the bridge is Willis' Lock and a keeper's cottage. Beyond this is the site of the Woolsthorpe Wharf where, for a brief period before the railway was opened, iron ore from Brewers Grave was loaded on to narrowboats *en route* to Stanton Ironworks at Ilkeston.

The old railway now crosses the canal by means of a low bridge and towpathers have to make their way up the steps to the right, on to the line and back down the other side. Here, virtually immediately, is Woolsthorpe Top Lock. In the spring of 1991, the Grantham Canal Restoration Society started restoration work on this lock by dewatering it and digging out some 5 ft of sludge, a prerequisite to assessing the amount of work that will be needed to reopen the structure.

The line continues on to go under Longmore Bridge which is closely followed by two more problematic bridges: Casthorpe Bridle Bridge and Casthorpe Bridge itself. The latter, which carries a minor road from Sedgebrook to Denton, is the centre of a campaign by the restoration society. The aim is to persuade Lincolnshire County Council to raise the height of the bridge sufficiently to make some 3 miles of this eastern end of the waterway navigable. It is the focus of attention because it is the last obstruction to navigation between here and the end of the canal near Grantham. The use of this section of the waterway has been stimulated by the provision of picnic sites and, just before the next bridge, a slipway to allow small craft to be launched on to the canal.

Within a ¼ mile a feeder from the Denton reservoir enters the canal on the

right-hand bank. The reservoir feeds the top pound of the canal from a sixty-one
million gallon supply just a couple of hundred yards to the right. Even though
the canal has been unused since the 1930s both feeder reservoirs (this and
Knipton) are in good condition and still supply water to the canal. Shortly after
the feeder the line passes a winding hole, bends right and then left to enter the
Harlaxton cutting. Here the canal is overhung by sultry willow trees and the
whole character of the line alters. The waterway is notably narrower than
hitherto and for many years after the opening of the eastern canal in February
1797 only one boat could pass through the cutting at a time. Luxury came in
1801 when two passing spaces were added.

The canal goes under Harlaxton Bridge mid-cutting to reach the site of
Harlaxton Wharf (on the right-hand bank) and then on to Vincent's Bridge.
After this last bridge, the cutting gradually fades away and the view opens out to
reveal the dual carriageways of the A1 trunk road riding high on an
embankment directly across the line of the canal. As we approach the road, it
becomes clear that here is a restorer's nightmare. This major road, effectively
equivalent to a motorway, acts as a very effective dam and the waterway channel
is culverted for some 300 yd through both the bypass and the slip-road which
runs beyond it. The cost of driving a new tunnel through the embankment
would be prohibitive even if the Department of Transport would allow such a

The problems faced by
restorers are no better
exemplified than by the
A1 embankment on the
Grantham Canal

venture. Various schemes have been devised because of this. The prime option is that a new basin (apparently with the suggested name of the Jessop Basin) be built on this side of the A1. This would leave a short stretch of water on the Grantham side which would then be made into a kind of linear water park. However, all hope of continuing the line on to Grantham has not been abandoned. Plans to widen the A1 may necessitate some rebuilding of the embankment and may yet allow a tunnel to be built through the line. Watch that space!

For the moment towpathers have to take a slightly devious route to reach Grantham. Having reached the embankment, turn right to pass over the culvert and on to the A607 road. Here turn left to go under the A1 bridge and on past the squash courts to the A1 slip-road which goes left. Turn left along here to reach a roundabout. Cross the road towards a hotel and pass down the left-hand side of the canal which has reappeared from its culvert for the final stretch into Grantham. The towpath is now broad, dry and well-made as it passes between some recent housing and a series of industrial units. It finally ends at Earle's Field Bridge where the view from the far side of the road is of a car park. Formerly the line continued on from here for about 500–600 yd to the town wharf. To return to the station, turn right along Earle's Field Lane to the A607 where you should turn left to continue to the railway bridge. Here Wharf Road crosses the A607. The site of the old basin was to the left but is now privately owned and not accessible. Turn right after going under the railway bridge to reach the station or straight on for the centre of town.

Further Explorations

As the entire 33 miles of the Grantham Canal is open for walking, if not boating, it should in theory be swarming with towpathers. However, the dearth of public transport makes the organization of one-way walks tricky. Grantham enthusiasts should therefore consider the possibility of short two-way walks, circular routes that make the most of the highly convoluted line, or a two-car trick with some like-minded fellows.

Having visited the eastern (Grantham) end of the line, you may like to walk the western end. The line can be followed using a combination of OS Landranger 129 (Nottingham & Loughborough) and Chris Cove-Smith's guide to the canal (available from the restoration society). For two-car trickers one suggested route of 8 miles runs from Cropwell Bishop, a small village off the A46 about $7\frac{1}{2}$ miles south-east of Nottingham city centre, to the River Trent.

The walk starts at Cropwell Town Bridge. Here the canal runs through an area of extensive gypsum quarrying, a rock that has caused a number of problems in maintaining the canal bed. There always were difficulties in keeping the line in water along this stretch (William Jessop came in for a fair amount of criticism because of it) and there is a 2 mile long dry section to this day. However, the course of the canal can still be followed without difficulty.

The 20 mile pound from Woolsthorpe comes to an end just after Cropwell Bishop with a spate of eight locks in under 3 miles (three 'Fosse' locks and a further five at the colliery village of Cotgrave). Polser Brook, the possible future route of the canal to the Trent at Holme Pierrepont, runs off to the right from the canal after the last lock in this series.

The current line continues westwards across Thurlbeck Aqueduct and past Nottingham airport to West Bridgford. Here towpathers have to scale the heights (and the hazardous crossing) of the A52 ring road embankment before descending to pass two locks. A little further on the canal disappears for a while under a road junction. If you maintain your course and aim for the floodlights of the Nottingham Forest football ground, you will shortly be able to rejoin the canal and to reach the River Trent at the aptly named Trent Lock. For those wanting to get into central Nottingham, turn left and cross the Trent at the bridge. This road (the A606) will take you into the city centre.

Further Information

The Grantham Canal Restoration Society has been pressing the case for the line for many years but they now appear to be gathering steam and what was once a dream could become reality. Undaunted by the not-inconsiderable task ahead of them, the society is enthusiastic and would welcome the membership of anyone willing to help further the restoration of this fine waterway. Those interested should contact:

Roger Cook,
28 Kendal Road,
Cropwell Bishop,
Nottinghamshire,
NG12 3DX.

The society sells (for a modest sum which goes to funds) a brief history and guide to the canal:
Cove-Smith, C., *The Grantham Canal Today*. 1974.

Although this covers the history of the line, further information about this and the other canals in the Nottingham area can be found in:
Hadfield, Charles, *The Canals of the East Midlands*. David & Charles, 1966.

6
THE LEICESTER LINE

Market Harborough to Foxton

Introduction

The hill at Foxton has become one of the most popular sights on the whole canal network and it's not hard to see why. The waterway interest is intense and accessible. There's a nice view. There's a place to eat and drink. There's plenty of activity. And there's 'fun for all the family'. Of course, this can have its negative side. Blackpool beach could be less crowded on some summer Sundays. Odd then that just a couple of hundred yards to the north, south or east, the Leicester line is one of the most peaceful and remote of any in the country.

The Leicester line is, strictly speaking, an integral part of the Grand Union Canal, a line that runs from London to Birmingham along one arm and to Leicester along the other. The Leicester branch started life as a series of wholly independent lines that began, in the south, at a junction with the former Grand Junction Canal at Norton, just 1 or 2 miles to the north-east of Daventry. From there the canal follows the M1 to pass the Watford services to reach the seven Watford Locks. After the 1,528 yd long Crick Tunnel, the canal continues north along a highly convoluted course past Yelvertoft and through the empty Northamptonshire farmland. It enters Leicestershire while crossing an aqueduct near Welford. Here a short arm leaves the main line for Welford Wharf just outside the centre of town. After passing through another tunnel (1,170 yd), the canal winds past Husbands Bosworth and heads north-east to reach Foxton, with its flight of ten locks and the remains of its famous canal lift. At the bottom of the flight a 5 mile long branch leaves for Market Harborough, while the main line bends north-west and goes through the 880 yd long Saddington Tunnel to pass down a long chain of locks to reach Blaby to the south of Leicester. It is now just a short distance to the centre of the city. The line curves around the south-western suburbs and then heads north to join the River Soar Navigation at West Bridge. After this, the river navigation takes the line to join the River Trent near Nottingham, a total distance from Norton Junction of 66 miles.

Don't be put off by the crowds. Foxton is worth visiting and, after all, you won't see a soul along most of the walk.

History

For at least a century the good people of Leicester had eyed the River Soar as a potential trading route to Nottingham, the River Trent and all ports north. But from 1634, when Charles I gave them permission, nearly a century and a half passed before the waterway was converted into a navigable route. Even then it was on an initiative from Loughborough, approximately 10 miles to the north of Leicester and 9 miles (by river) south of the Trent. An Act was passed in April 1776 and the canalized Soar was opened from the Trent to Loughborough just two years later.

The navigation was soon returning a good profit and by 1780 was providing its promoters with a 5 per cent dividend. Cargo, which included coal from the Erewash Canal, was taken up the Soar and transhipped for onward road carriage. The success of the line was noticed in Leicester and the idea of extending the navigation was again raised. This time action was taken. An Act of 1791 authorized the extension of the Soar navigation for a further 16 miles and the line was formally opened in October 1794.

The success of the Soar Navigation and the arrival of canal mania soon stimulated talk about taking the line even further south. At a meeting in Market Harborough in 1792, the possibility of a canal from Leicester to the town was discussed. Such was the enthusiasm of local tradesfolk and dignitaries, and the over-optimism that typified the period, that the meeting soon got around to extending the line to Northampton where the new canal, it was said, could link up with the River Nene as well as with the new Grand Junction Canal. These links, it was agreed, would open up trade to London and the east.

An initial survey was carried out by Christopher Staveley who, quite sensibly, divided the project into two halves: Leicester to Market Harborough and Market Harborough to Northampton. In the summer of 1792, William Jessop was appointed engineer and John Varley was engaged to carry out a more detailed survey. By this time the Grand Junction Canal had already decided to build its own branch to Northampton and the Nene. It was clearly prudent not to build another line into Northampton and Varley decided simply to form a junction with the GJC instead. This had the additional benefit of providing more direct access to London.

The final proposal for what was to be the Leicestershire & Northamptonshire

Union Canal (popularly known as the Old Union) took the Soar navigation from Leicester to Aylestone and then cut a canal via Saddington, Foxton, Theddingworth, East Farndon, Kelmarsh and Maidwell on to Hardingstone and the GJC. This was a line of about 44 miles plus a branch of 4 miles from Lubenham to Market Harborough. The main construction work was to be in the form of four tunnels: Saddington (880 yd), Foxton (1,056 yd), Kelmarsh (990 yd) and Great Oxendon (286 yd). This plan was accepted by the promoters and was duly passed by Parliament on 30 April 1793, the same day as the GJC Act. The Old Union was authorized to raise £200,000 plus a further £100,000 if needed.

Activity started at West Bridge, Leicester. In October 1794, the canal was opened to Blaby, just over 5 miles to the south. By March 1795, the line had moved 3 miles closer to Market Harborough but already there were financial and labour problems. The company had great difficulty in obtaining funds from its shareholders and this shortage was beginning to affect its work. There were also pressures from local landowners who demanded inflated prices for the land required by the canal company. Although Saddington Tunnel was started in July 1795, the committee decided in the autumn to curtail its ambitions by only taking the line as far as Gumley, 3 miles short of Market Harborough. With the problems they already had, it must have come as a serious blow to discover that Saddington Tunnel had not been built straight and needed some expensive rebuilding at several places to allow wide vessels to pass through. By 7 April 1797, 17 miles of broad canal, from Leicester to Debdale Wharf near Gumley, was open for traffic. For over twelve years this was the southernmost terminal of the canal. It was not until October 1809 that the line finally reached Market Harborough which was by now officially recognized as the terminus. The Old Union had cost £205,000 and, despite the failure to reach the GJC, the opening of the line was celebrated at the Angel in Market Harborough with a fine dinner for all the local VIPs involved.

The route to the south wasn't totally forgotten however. By June 1808 the GJC saw the potential for an alternative route east of Birmingham to Manchester and actively supported a meeting in London where a new line was discussed. Benjamin Bevan was asked to consider the many routes that had already been proposed and to pick the most appropriate. He chose a route which passed through Foxton, Welford and Crick to join the Oxford Canal at Braunston. However, as the GJC were involved they applied pressure for a direct link with them and the route was altered so that the two lines met at Norton. It was this route that received parliamentary approval in May 1810 under the title of the Grand Union Act together with authorization to raise £245,000 with £50,000 more if required. The proposed line included a branch to the village of Welford. The required sums were, perhaps surprisingly, quickly raised and Bevan was appointed engineer.

The work began on the Grand Union (now known as the Old Grand Union to avoid confusion with the present GU) at Foxton where ten locks in two staircases of five were built to take the line up to its summit pound. These were opened on 1 October 1812 by which time the line had reached Husbands Bosworth Tunnel. The 1,170 yd long tunnel was finished in May 1813 and the line opened as far as Stanford, 10 miles south of Foxton and just over 13 miles from Norton.

Problems arose in 1812 at Crick where the proposed tunnel was found to pass through an area of quicksand. Bevan was forced to revise the line through an even longer tunnel to the east. This was compensated for by the avoidance of a tunnel at Watford where the line was diverted through a private park following a suitable compensation agreement with the local landowner.

The Old Grand Union as opened on 9 August 1814 was just over 23 miles long with seventeen locks. The locks were built to a narrowboat gauge, although all the tunnels and bridges were built to a broad barge width. The line from Market Harborough had cost £292,000.

By 1812, the Old Union Canal was already paying its investors dividends and the line had a steady volume of local traffic. Dividends reached the peak of 6 per cent in 1837 although, as was the case with most canals, levels declined from then on. The Old Grand Union, however, was never a real success. The expected through traffic was not as great as forecast and it wasn't until 1827 that the first dividend was paid. Even by 1840, the dividend was still only $1\frac{3}{4}$ per cent.

It was inevitable that the two lines would work together and, by 1863, co-operation was such that the two companies were as good as one. At this time the canal carrying company Fellows, Morton & Clayton operated steamers between London and Leicester with Boots the Chemists in Nottingham as an important customer. Fly-boats were able to do the trip between London and Leicester in just three days. There were also fly-boats operating from Market Harborough.

By the 1890s the Leicester line as a whole (i.e. the Old Union and Old Grand Union Canals) was beginning to deteriorate and the companies were virtually bankrupt. Through coal traffic had declined from 125,000 tons p.a. in the 1850s to around 5,000 tons and comments were widely made that trade could only improve if the canals were dredged and the locks on the Old Grand Union widened. The chief protagonists in this were Fellows, Morton & Clayton who suggested that both canals should be bought out by the Grand Junction Canal Company and then modernized. This it duly did, following an Act of 1894, for a price of approximately £17,000.

The GJC immediately implemented a dredging programme and negotiated lower tolls with the navigation companies to the north. In fact, the GJC guaranteed toll levels to the Leicester and Loughborough Navigations and to the Erewash Canal. This agreement later converted to an option to buy the three in 1897. The GJC also decided, with prompting from Fellows, Morton & Clayton, to improve the Watford and Foxton Locks. The argument that was forwarded said that wider locks would enable the carriers to operate larger vessels, reduce carrying costs and increase traffic.

The GJC took a radical approach to the problem at Foxton. Here it decided to replace the ten locks with an inclined plane lift which would take a 70 ton barge or two narrow boats up and down the hill. The plane was developed by Gordon Thomas who built a test model at Bulbourne. The system consisted of two counterbalancing watertight tanks, resting on carriages that ran on rails. Power was supplied by means of a steam engine. Construction work started on the site early in 1898 and the incline was open for traffic in July 1900 at a cost of £37,500. Appropriately, the first working boat through was a Fellows, Morton & Clayton steamer. The lift had the benefit of taking around twelve minutes to pass up the hill compared with about an hour for the locks. It also saved a considerable volume of water, an important commodity along a line which suffered during periods of drought.

A similar plane was considered as a replacement for the seven Watford locks but the capital and running costs involved dissuaded the company from proceeding. Instead it was thought that the Watford locks should be widened. The decision to go ahead was never made and they were merely refurbished as narrow locks during the winter of 1901. During the course of 1900, the

The Foxton inclined-plane lift in about 1905. This view shows the upper docks and the engine house, now the site of the trust's museum. The caissons went down the hill to the right

British Waterways

The newly completed Foxton inclined-plane lift is here being inspected by a group of dignitaries as the northern caisson descends into the lower canal arm

British Waterways

company also dropped its options to take over the Loughborough and Leicester Navigations and the Erewash Canal. The increase in traffic promised by Fellows, Morton & Clayton simply hadn't materialized and the company must have been losing faith in the Leicester line. This situation culminated in the closure of the Foxton lift. The cost of maintaining the engine in steam together with the three members of staff needed to operate the works simply made the otherwise splendid structure uneconomic. Although the incline remained in place until 1926, it was unused after March 1911. These attempts at reinvigorating the Leicester line had cost the GJC nearly £80,000 and there had been little return for its money.

From 1910, when 40,767 tons of cargo passed through Foxton, trade went into a gradual and then dramatic decline with the greater competition from the railways. By 1924, less than 10,000 tons went along the Leicester line although the mainline GJC traffic from London to Birmingham had remained good. In 1925 the company was again considering ways of expanding its traffic and a plan was launched to take over the three Warwick Canals (the Warwick & Birmingham, the Warwick & Napton and the Birmingham & Warwick Junction Canal) as well as the Regent's Canal. Following the passage of an approval Act, the

Grand Union Canal Co. Ltd, which incorporated all these lines (and later the Leicester and Loughborough Navigations and the Erewash Canal), came into being on 1 January 1928.

The new Grand Union started with vigour, as befits a youngster, and plans were made to widen the Foxton and Watford Locks. As a grant was refused by the government, the scheme was dropped and all thoughts of restoring trade to pre-First World War levels were forgotten. Some coal and timber traffic still took the line (some seventy pairs of narrowboats a week passed through Foxton during the Second World War) but by the time of nationalization in 1948 this had virtually stopped. By 1968, the Leicester line was scheduled for abandonment and was only rescued by the Transport Act which designated it as a cruiseway suitable for pleasure boat use. It remains this today.

The Walk

Start and Finish: Market Harborough Basin (OS ref: SP 727879)
Distance: 9½ miles/15 km
Map: OS Landranger 141 (Kettering & Corby)
Car park: At the basin (near The Six Packs pub) or in a lay-by just a little further along the A6 towards Leicester
Public transport: BR Market Harborough on Leicester to London line

The first part of this walk goes along the towpath with a shorter return cross-country. The footpaths on the return journey are accessible but appear to be little used and can become obscured and overgrown. This is particularly the case in late summer. If you want to return along the towpath, this will extend the walk to 12 miles. A second alternative is to catch the Midland Red Fox bus which runs sporadically between Foxton and Market Harborough. Do enquire first on (0533) 313391. A third alternative is to skip the walk entirely and simply to visit the Foxton Locks from the Leicester County Council car park. This is signposted from the A427 at Lubenham.

The full walk begins at The Six Packs pub on the main road out of Market Harborough towards Leicester. An unmetalled track leads to the Market Harborough Basin where there are a number of boatyards in various states of disrepair. The towpath begins by passing to the left and around the back of the old Harborough Marine buildings before setting off between the back gardens of Market Harborough suburbia.

The canal to Market Harborough is in truth no more than a branch although at one time it was planned to be part of the main line. If that plan had been instigated the canal would have continued beyond the Harborough Basin along

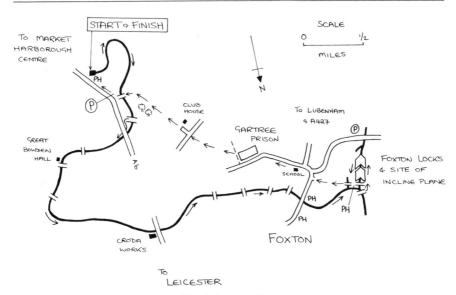

The Leicester line

the Welland Valley past Lubenham and on to Northampton. In the event the line to Market Harborough was built as a terminus when the old Leicestershire & Northamptonshire Union Company ran out of money in 1809. The line then became a branch when the proposal from the company's engineer, John Barnes, was enacted and the main line was taken up a flight of locks at Foxton to join the Grand Junction Canal at Norton.

Although it looks a little drab these days, the basin at Market Harborough was the venue of the 1950 Inland Waterways Association national rally. The event was not only the first of its kind and a major focus for the developing canal restoration movement but was also the scene of one of the more notorious incidents in the row between Tom Rolt and Robert Aickman. Those who enjoy a good gossip should read David Bolton's and/or Tom Rolt's books on the event (see below).

The canal makes a huge loop around the houses to the right. At intervals the line narrows to stop-plank grooves or sites of missing swing bridges. After going around the loop, the canal bends sharply left to reach a small footbridge. Those returning cross-country will see this again. At the next bridge, go underneath and then up left to cross the canal to the right-hand bank. The line now enters a shallow cutting to go under the A6. This cutting then deepens to about 40 ft before reaching the fine arched Saunt's Bridge. After a sharp bend the canal leads to Bowden Hall hidden amid the trees on the right. Go under Bowden Hall Bridge, with its associated pipe, and continue along an increasingly overgrown towpath to another bridge and a bend left.

The canal now stands above the valley to the right where a tributary of the Welland winds its way east. From here on we can enjoy a steady, quiet walk through butterfly and bird rich arable land to reach the slightly incongruous Croda factory. At one time the factory rendered animal bones into meal and tallow. From the bridge (Gallows Hill Bridge) the canal winds around the contours to a brick-arch bridge, followed by a fenced off spill weir that takes surplus water down to the river. After passing under a footbridge the village of Foxton can be seen through the hedge to the right. Just before the following bridge a post indicates that there is just 1 mile to the Leicester (Grand Union) main line.

The canal now swings to the right to reach the Foxton swing bridge and Foxton Bridge. Just after this latter bridge a gap in the hedge to the right gives access to Foxton village where there are two pubs and a shop. The Black Horse, which is visible from the canal, can be reached by walking up to the road and turning right. The Shoulder of Mutton, meanwhile, can be reached by turning

View up the Foxton flight
of ten locks on the
Leicester line

left down the slight hill. The small supermarket is further down the hill after The Shoulder of Mutton.

Back on the towpath, there is now just a short stroll before the entire character of the walk changes. If here on a weekend or during the summer months, prepare yourselves! The first sign is that the canal becomes crowded with moored boats as we reach the bottom of the Foxton flight. This is first seen on the left with a small bridge that passes over a canal arm. This arm, which is now a private mooring spot, was once the bottom entrance of the Foxton inclined plane, a canal lift mechanism which replaced the locks for a period early in the twentieth century. More of this later. The towpath, meanwhile, continues onwards to Foxton Junction where the Harborough arm joins the main line.

On the left is the complex of buildings which surround the old wharf at the bottom of the Foxton flight. Originally the buildings included a carpenter's shop, a blacksmith's forge and the offices of the canal company as well as the old lock house. Nowadays there is a pub (Bridge 61), a shop and a boat yard. In addition, on a warm day, there will be, quite literally, hundreds of people swarming all over the locks and the remains of the inclined plane. On the canal, meanwhile, there will be some highly confused boaters who, having gotten used to the solitude of the rest of the Leicester line, have suddenly arrived at the canal equivalent of Trafalgar Square. Perhaps more alarmingly from their point of view they also find themselves to be the centre of attention as they attempt to take their craft up the ten locks.

Continue round the towpath to reach the roving bridge and cross the main line. From the bridge there is a fine view to the left up the flight of locks that climb the Foxton hill up to the lock-keeper's cottage at the top. At the bottom a small brick bridge goes over the first lock. To reach it continue over the roving bridge and walk onward towards the locks.

Although paths go virtually everywhere, take the towpath that runs up the right-hand side of the locks. The Foxton flight consists of two staircases of five chambers each. A staircase is simply a set of locks in which the top gate of one acts as the bottom gate of the next. Clearly it is not possible for boats to pass in this kind of set up, so boats are well organized by the resident lock-keeper and there is a convenient central pound where boats can pass each other. Each lock is provided with a large side pound into which water is passed when a lock is evacuated. These can be seen over to the left. These provide extra water to each lock thereby avoiding complete drainage of the system at any one point.

After a stroll up to the lock cottage at the top of the flight, cross the canal at the lock bridge and pass down slightly left to go along a clear path in between two of the side pounds. This path is part of the inclined plane trail and leads around to the top of the incline. To the left is what remains of the old boilerhouse (now converted into a museum) and to the right are the remains of the top lock and the slope itself with its rail grooves still largely in position.

The inclined plane at Foxton was built to reduce the amount of time taken to pass up and down the slope and to reduce the substantial loss of water down the hill. A boat using the incline could be moved up or down the 75 ft in twelve minutes, compared with forty-five to sixty minutes for passage along the locks, and with no loss of water from the upper pound.

The system, which was engineered by Gordon Cale Thomas, consisted of two 307 ft long parallel slopes, with a gradient of 1 in 4, on which ran huge tanks or caissons, each large enough to hold two narrowboats. The tanks were made of steel plates and were 80 ft long, 15 ft wide and 5 ft deep. They weighed about 250 tons each and were supported on eight wheels which ran on four rails that went up and down the slope. The position of the rails is still visible on the incline and a small section of the track (which turns out to be identical to that used on Brunel's Great Western) has been fitted into place, together with an explanatory notice.

The lift was operated by having the tanks on the two slopes linked by a steel wire rope so that they counterbalanced each other and thereby reduced the amount of effort needed to move them. The power needed to overcome the inertia was provided by a steam engine: a double-cylinder, high pressure jet condensing type steamed using two 'Lancashire' boilers, one of which was kept in reserve. The engine was coupled to the tanks by a 7 in steel wire haulage rope which passed over a winding drum in the engine house. The ropes were carried on rollers which were set into the face of the planes – an example of which can be seen further down the hill.

At the bottom of the incline, the tanks simply sank into the lower canal arm and the boats floated in or out. At the top, the situation was a little more complex. Here the tanks fitted flush into a lock and were then forced against it by means of steam-powered hydraulic rams which applied their pressure through buffers at the other end. This, hopefully, produced a water-tight seal. To seal the system during use, the tanks and the docks were fitted with guillotine gates at each end.

After two years work by the contractors, Messrs. J. & H. Gwynne of Hammersmith, the lift was opened on 10 July 1900 at a cost of £37,500 including the price of the land. Three men were employed to work the lift: one on the steam engine and one each to operate the top and bottom gates. For the first six months, the lift cost about £1 4s. 6d. a day to run, the main expenses being manpower and coal. With full use this worked out at about one twentieth of a penny per ton of cargo.

When working, the system was a good one but in the long run the plane was not a success. The key mechanical problem was that the rails repeatedly gave way under the weight of the tanks. In retrospect it was said that they were never seated properly. The $\frac{3}{4}$ in bolts regularly snapped and the rails subsided. This, surely, was a problem that could have been solved but the main reason for the failure of the lift was that the traffic over the Leicester line was too irregular to justify the cost of maintaining the engine in steam and of paying the staff.

The northern hill of the Foxton inclined plane on the Leicester line

In 1909, the locks were reinstated, initially to allow traffic to pass at night when the plane wasn't working. But on 26 October 1910 it was announced that the plane was to be abandoned and that all traffic was to use the locks. Although the plane was used sporadically thereafter, it was last operated in March 1911. Maintenance continued until 1914 during which time various alternative methods of powering and working the incline were considered. But in 1914 the dismantling work began. The boilers were removed and the chimney demolished between 1920 and 1924. The demolition was finally completed in 1927–8 when what was left was sold for scrap. One boat load is said to have sunk in the lower arm and apparently could be seen for many years sticking out of the water.

Part of the old engine house has been rebuilt and now contains the Foxton Canal Museum. Here the Foxton Inclined Plane Trust have their various artefacts including a range of photographs and a working model. Entrance to the museum is by donation.

From the top of the incline, take the path that goes down to the left of the main slope. This passes one of the railway carts that was used during the construction of the plane and an original rope pulley. The brick bridge at the bottom of the hill goes over the canal arm which runs to the bottom of the incline. The arm has been privately owned since 1969 and is now used for residential mooring. Cross the bridge and follow the unmetalled lane out to the

Tyrley Locks on the Birmingham & Liverpool Junction Canal

Canal buildings at the bottom of the Foxton Locks on the Leicester line

The northern portal of Telford's Harecastle Tunnel on the Trent & Mersey Canal

The Worcester & Birmingham Canal Society plaque commemorating the meeting of Tom Rolt and Robert Aickman at Tardebigge on the Worcester & Birmingham Canal

Kidderminster Locks and St Mary and All Saints Church, Kidderminster on the Staffordshire &
Worcestershire Canal

Kidderminster gas works on the Staffordshire & Worcestershire Canal

Trevor Basin on the Llangollen Canal

Narrowboats crossing Pont Cysyllte Aqueduct on the Llangollen Canal

road. If you wish to revisit Foxton (for the pubs, shop, bus stop or towpath route back to Market Harborough), turn left. To take the shorter cross-country route, turn right.

Follow this minor road around left (ignore the turning to the right) and keep straight on past a junction where a road sign points right to Market Harborough. This quiet country lane passes a school and then, most dramatically, Gartree prison. As the prison buildings come to an end, a footpath sign on the left-hand verge of the road indicates right down a metalled track. Turn right to follow the lane to a point just before the main prison walls end. Across the grass verge, a stile takes the footpath into a field on the other side of which is a yellow-painted post which marks the line of the public right of way. The course between the two posts should now be continued straight on to pass to the left of a barbed wire fence and along the edge of another field. This leads to a metalled lane.

Continue on, maintaining the same straight course, to pass some huts (the home of a model aircraft club) and a clay pigeon shoot. With a hedge to the right, the path soon reaches a signpost which points in four directions (A6–A6–Lubenham–Foxton). Continue straight on (i.e. the same straight course that was originally set between the first stile and the yellow-painted post) to pass to the right of a short stand of copper beech trees. From here the line of the canal, as it winds around the suburbs of Market Harborough, can be seen ahead and to the right. If the original straight course is maintained, you will soon reach the canal embankment and, a short distance further on, a gap in the hedge up to the footbridge passed earlier. Cross the canal and follow the lane out to a lay-by. Turn right to reach the main Market Harborough–Leicester road. Turn right to walk back to The Six Packs. The short stroll back to the pub isn't wholly dull. Just outside the Knoll is a Grand Junction Canal Company boundary post marking the extent of the company's property surrounding the canal basin.

Further Explorations

The towpath on the Leicester line is often impassable and unwelcoming to walkers. It is passable, however, in the area of the Watford Locks and these are well worth a return stroll of about 1¼ miles from the B4036 just off the A5 near the M1 at Watford (Northamptonshire).

The canal at Watford is nervously wedged between the M1 on one side and the A5 and the main Euston–Rugby railway on the other. Park near the M1 bridge which is next to the appropriately named Watford Gap motorway service station. The towpath starts near the Stag's Head restaurant and takes the right-hand bank. The good, grassy path leads around to the locks which are announced by a brick pumping station, a set of stop planks and a bridge which proclaims to have been rebuilt in 1976. The first lock and the lock-keeper's cottage follow. The line then bends slightly right amid a rich thicket of trees to reach a staircase of four locks before reaching a wide pound, the top lock, a British Waterways hut and the M1 bridge.

The Watford Locks raise the line by just over 52 ft. As part of the scheme of improvements that brought about the Foxton Incline, there were plans to replace the Watford flight with a similar lift system. However, even before the Foxton Incline was open, the plan was dropped in favour of upgrading the locks. They were consequently partially rebuilt during the winter of 1901–2 but a scheme to widen them was abandoned and an inclined plane was not considered again.

After a brief picnic by the staircase, return along the towpath to the B4036 and the car.

Further Information

The Foxton Inclined Plane Trust not only runs the museum but fully intends to restore the lift to its former glory. The trust was formed in 1980 and membership is open to anyone interested in the plane and who wants to help in any way. They can be contacted at:

Foxton Inclined Plane Trust Ltd,
Bottom Lock,
Foxton,
Market Harborough,
Leicestershire,
LE16 7RA.

The Department of Planning & Transportation Leicestershire County Council in association with the trust publishes two books that are crammed with information about the lift and the canal:
Foxton Locks and Inclined Plane. 1985.
Foxton Locks and the Grand Junction Canal Co. 1988.
Both are available in the museum or in the bottom lock shop.

The history of the Leicester lines are included in:
Faulkner, Alan H., *The Grand Junction Canal.* David & Charles, 1973.

For details of the success of and conflicts surrounding the 1950 IWA Market Harborough rally:
Bolton, David, *Race Against Time.* Mandarin Paperbacks, 1990.
Rolt, L.T.C., *Landscape with Canals.* Alan Sutton Publishing, 1977.

7
THE LLANGOLLEN CANAL
Chirk to Llangollen

Introduction

In many ways the Llangollen Canal was a bit of a failure. The original canal of which it was a part, the Ellesmere Canal, was intended to be a north–south line that joined the Rivers Mersey, Dee and Severn. Instead, it ended up being an east–west line that never really fulfilled any particular strategic function. But there again if failures are made like this then long may they be built!

The Llangollen Canal wasn't known as such until a British Waterways booklet was published in 1956. The Shropshire Union, of which it is really a part, consists of a line that runs from Autherley Junction (near Wolverhampton) to Ellesmere Port via Chester. What is more correctly known as the Llangollen branch leaves that main line at Hurleston, about $2\frac{1}{2}$ miles north-west of Nantwich. From there it passes through rural Cheshire before entering the remoter parts of Shropshire just north of Whitchurch at Grindley Brook. The land now seems even emptier as the canal turns south and west to go past the peatlands of Whixall Moss. After skirting around the southern edge of Ellesmere, the line reaches Frankton Junction. From here the Montgomery Canal once ran 35 miles to Newtown and, who knows, may do so once again within a few years. The Llangollen meanwhile turns north-west to reach Chirk where, half-way across a splendid aqueduct, the line enters Wales. After going through two tunnels, the canal passes over one of the most spectacular sights on the inland waterways network: the magnificent Pont Cysyllte Aqueduct. At the northern end, the canal passes Trevor Basin and turns abruptly west, reaching Llangollen 5 miles further on. It is now just 2 narrow miles to Llantisilio and the Horseshoe Falls, the feeder and beginning of the canal.

If anything can tempt the armchair towpather out of his seat then this walk must be it. The splendid scenery around Llangollen coupled with the incomparable Pont Cysyllte should be enough to get anyone up and going. There's none better. Do it!

History

A proposal for what became the Ellesmere Canal was originally advanced in 1789 by a group of Ruabon industrialists who sought an improved freight route to the Mersey. The plan, as launched to a public meeting at the Royal Oak Hotel in Ellesmere on 31 August 1791, was a grand one: a north–south route to link the Rivers Mersey, Dee and Severn. The line that was agreed ran from the Mersey at Netherpool (now known as Ellesmere Port) to the Dee at Chester and thence via Overton to the Severn at Shrewsbury. Branches were proposed to Ruabon and Llangollen, to Llanymynech and possibly to Whitchurch and Wem. Progress was agreed and the line was surveyed by two local men, William Turner of Whitchurch and John Duncombe of Oswestry. They estimated the cost of the new canal to be £171,098 of which about two-thirds would be for the branches.

There clearly must have been some debate as to whether the two local lads were up to the job for not long after, following a suggestion from John Smeaton, the promoters called in William Jessop, whom they described as 'an Engineer of approved Character and Experience', to proffer more learned advice. He duly reported back in August 1792. The Jessop line followed the original route to Chester but then it ran to Wrexham and Ruabon, through a 4,607 yd long tunnel, over an aqueduct at Pont Cysyllte through a tunnel to Chirk and then on to Shrewsbury. Jessop was man enough to draw attention to the difficulties with the terrain but he proposed the line at £176,898 or £196,898 if branches to Llanymynech and Holt were added.

Reassured by Jessop's considerations, the promoters tested the financial waters. In September 1792, subscriptions were invited and, as the country was amid canal mania, the response was overwhelming. Some 1,234 subscribers from as far afield as Derby and Leicester offered a total of £967,700. The company had the welcome problem of having to scale down the bids to accept just £246,500. The Ellesmere Canal was under way.

On 30 April 1793, the Act was passed to authorize a narrow canal (originally it was to be a broad line but this was changed during the passage of the bill in order to save money) with powers to raise funds of £400,000 plus £100,000 more if required. A number of amendments were added during the course of the bill including one which took the route along a slightly higher level near Ruabon to avoid the necessity of the tunnel. William Jessop was appointed engineer with Duncombe, Turner and Thomas Denson as assistants. This team was later, and most notably, extended when a young Thomas Telford was appointed as 'General agent, surveyor, engineer, architect and overlooker of the works'.

Work on the Ellesmere Canal began on the Wirral line in November 1788. By 1 July 1795, packet-boats were passing up and down its $8\frac{3}{4}$ miles and the line soon became both a busy and popular route. For a shilling passengers could ride between Ellesmere Port and Chester and be served with tea and cakes while doing so. Perhaps more importantly from the canal's point of view, the first coal boats from the Mersey arrived at Tower Wharf, Chester, in early 1796. Toll revenue was coming in!

Meanwhile, on what is now the Llangollen Canal, cutting started somewhat later and at various points along the line. In 1794, work started at Hordley, near Frankton, moving westwards towards Llanymynech (on what is now known as the Montgomery Canal). The aim was to gain access to the limestone quarries at Llanymynech. The 11 miles from Frankton to Carreghofa (24 miles short of the Montgomery terminus at Newtown) were completed in the autumn of 1796.

At Fron Cysyllte, near Llangollen, the challenge to span the River Dee was both daunting and exciting. The original proposal was to lock the canal down the valley to an aqueduct 50 ft above the Dee. This design was in keeping with the technology and experience available to engineers at the time. The relatively junior Thomas Telford, who had been asked merely to produce the working drawings, did not approve of this rather unambitious project. He had recently had experience of working with Thomas Eyton on the iron Longdon-on-Tern Aqueduct on the Shrewsbury Canal and he suggested that a similar structure could be used at Fron Cysyllte. He argued that it would be just as cheap for the company to use embankments to carry the line to an iron trough which would then take the canal across the valley on 125 ft high stone pillars. It was a bold and risky suggestion but the flair and imagination which it encompassed was there to be recognized. Clearly Jessop and the committee agreed and approval was gained almost immediately. On 25 July 1795, the foundation stone for the aqueduct was laid by Richard Myddleton, the local MP. Ten years later the great aqueduct was opened with the due pomp and ceremony that befits a monument to the genius that built it. Even today, Pont Cysyllte is impressive and it is no wonder that Sir Walter Scott described it as the greatest work of art he'd ever seen.

During the course of the Pont Cysyllte construction work, efforts were made to take the line from Chirk to Weston. Work started on the Hordley to Weston section separately from the Hordley to Chirk stretch and was finished earlier, in 1797. The whole stretch was navigable in 1801 when Chirk Aqueduct, a fine structure that would receive considerably more attention if it wasn't for its neighbour, was opened.

With all this activity in the centre of the line, it was now time to begin on the problematical course north from Ruabon to Chester. Telford was given the job of re-surveying the route and, following some minor brushes with local landowners, had his proposals approved by Jessop and authorized by a new Act of 1796. From Pont Cysyllte, the Telford line rose 76 ft by locks to Plas Kynaston and then ran level past Ruabon and Bersham towards Chester.

A narrowboat waits at Black Park Basin near Chirk where cargo was transhipped to and from the Glyn Valley Tramway. The railway was an important wharf for local collieries and for the granite and slate quarries along the valley. It was removed in 1935

D. Llewellyn Davies, British Waterways

Construction work started in June of 1796 and about $2\frac{1}{2}$ miles of the line was built between Moss and Gwersyllt.

By 1800, the formidable terrain, coupled with the difficult economic situation in the midst of the Napoleonic Wars, had rendered the northern venture financially impossible. Jessop was forced to report to his committee that it was now wholly inadvisable to build a canal between Pont Cysyllte and Chester, and further progress was stopped. This, of course, left the company in a position where it had a series of odd bits of canal totally detached from the rest of the system and even from its key objective of the Rivers Dee and Mersey.

A cheaper route into Chester was therefore sought and this was calculated as being one which struck eastwards from Frankton to the Chester Canal at Hurleston near Nantwich. The branch to Whitchurch had already been started in February 1797, so all that was needed was a connecting stretch between Whitchurch and Hurleston. This was agreed and work began in November 1802. The line to Whitchurch was finished in 1804 and the line to Hurleston was finally ready on 25 March 1805. The continuing line to Shrewsbury was never completed.

The decision to continue building Pont Cysyllte Aqueduct was a difficult one; what was once the main north–south line now merely took a small branch into the otherwise insignificant town of Trevor. The promoters must have taken a gamble on the carriage of coal from the Ruabon collieries and Telford clearly saw the importance of the Dee at Llantisilio as a water supply. We can only be thankful that they made the decision they did.

The Llangollen Canal from Hurleston to Trevor and to Weston appears to have been opened in late 1805. The first passage was recorded in the local press when five vessels from the Montgomery branch, all laden with oak timber, arrived at Tower Wharf in Chester. Once the connection had been made, trade grew rapidly with a flourishing business in coal, limestone, lime and building materials. The line as opened was 29 miles long from Hurleston to Frankton, with a further 11 miles to Pont Cysyllte and another six to the Llantisilio canal terminus. There are twenty-one locks altogether including six at Grindley Brook and four at Hurleston. The necessary water was obtained under an Act of 1804 which authorized a navigable feeder to be built from Trevor along the Vale of Llangollen to the Dee at Llantisilio. Here Telford built an impressive semi-circular weir known as the Horseshoe Falls. This feeder line, now a popular holiday route to Llangollen, was opened in early 1808.

On completion of the line, the company had raised £410,875 and received some £48,586 in tolls and other receipts. No dividends had yet been paid. Jessop had left in 1801. Telford, however, remained as part-time general agent with Thomas Denson as resident engineer.

There was no doubt that the Ellesmere Canal was going to be a moderately successful line but its dependency on the Chester Canal and the fact that it wasn't linked with the rest of the canal network always meant that its potential was limited. The company was clearly aware of this and, in order to ensure continuity, the Ellesmere attempted to take over the Chester in 1804. This attempt collapsed when the two parties could not agree on a suitable evaluation. By 1813, however, the Chester was heading towards a more stable financial state and further overtures from the Ellesmere were not so rebuffed. On 1 July 1813, the two companies merged to form the United Company of Proprietors of the Ellesmere and Chester Canals.

The future of the new company was always going to be limited by its lack of outlets to the south. Initially, the ECC paid court to the Trent & Mersey Canal Company suggesting a more tangible link at Middlewich. But the level of co-operation between the canal companies was inevitably low and the T & M refused as it was convinced that the EEC would take some of its own trade. Eventually, following the passage of the Birmingham & Liverpool Junction Canal Act, agreement was reached and the line from Barbridge to Wardle (near Middlewich) was opened in September 1833. This was soon followed by the B & LJ which forged a new line from Autherley, on the Staffordshire & Worcestershire near Wolverhampton, to the ECC at Nantwich on 2 March 1835 (for more information on the B & LJ see Chapter 2). The ECC now had two links with the canal network and prospects must have looked good.

Although there was an increase in trade, the opening of these routes to the south did not have the expected impact on activity along the Llangollen line. Limestone was carried from Llanymynech, coal from Chirk and iron from Ruabon but these all hit heavy competition from the quarries and collieries in the Midlands. As an example, of the 60,000 tons of iron carried by the ECC to Liverpool, only 11,000 came from North Wales, the rest coming from Staffordshire and Shropshire. And, as elsewhere, railway competition was beginning to bite.

It was this baring of teeth that prompted the next move. In May 1845, the ECC and B & LJ merged to form what was to become the Shropshire Union Railway and Canal Company. The plan was a bold one. In deference to the new age, the new company would convert their canals into railways. Their engineer, W.A. Provis, assured them that the cost of converting a canal to a railway was just half that of building a railway from scratch. This would provide them with a significant advantage over the many lines that were already springing up throughout the region and competing heavily for traffic. With this objective, the new Shropshire Union incorporated the Montgomery Canal and the Shrewsbury Canal, and took a lease on the Shropshire Canal. Work started not, interestingly enough, on a canal bed but on a line between Shrewsbury and Stafford. This was a joint venture with the Shrewsbury & Birmingham Railway that was seen as a quick solution which wouldn't involve any loss of trade on the operating canal lines.

This period of far-sightedness by the new SU seems to have been short-lived. By the autumn of 1846, the newly formed London and North Western Railway, seeing that the SU could become a serious competitor to its own activities, offered to lease the SU. Perhaps rather unimaginatively, the SU committee agreed. The Act authorizing the move was passed in June 1847. By July 1849 (by which time the Shrewsbury to Stafford line had opened), the LNWR had persuaded the SU to give up all thoughts of further railway building in return for having their debt serviced. With this, the SU's railway ambitions effectively evaporated.

Despite this, the SU's canal activities were thriving. In 1850, the revenue on the line was over £180,000 with a useful profit and a very vigorous carrying business. But the threat of increasing railway competition was being felt. From an operating surplus of £45,000 p.a. in the late 1840s, profits dropped to around £11,000 by the late 1860s even though the level of receipts were similar. The SU were forced to accept lower rates in the face of railway competition. An agreement with the Great Western Railway, for example, forced canal rates to below those of the railway for traffic to Llangollen, Ruabon and Chirk. At this time, most of the company's income was, in fact, from their canal carrying business rather than from tolls: in 1870 the company operated some 213 narrowboats of which fifty-six regularly plied the Llangollen line.

By now the profitability of the Llangollen Canal was becoming a cause for concern. In 1873, the new engineer, G.R. Jebb, even went to the lengths of suggesting that the line from Llangollen to Weston should be converted into a narrow gauge railway. Although reprieved, things did not improve. In the 1880s, a number of works near Pont Cysyllte began to close and by 1905 there was little coal or limestone being shipped from Chirk. By the time of the First World War, the canal as a whole was running at a loss and the LNWR saw no reason to keep it solvent. It forced the SU to make economies. On 1 June 1920, the SU announced that it was to give up the carrying business that still ran some 202 boats up and down the line. At the end of 1922, the SU company was absorbed by the LNWR which in turn was itself absorbed into the London Midland & Scottish Railway the following year.

In 1929, the canal as a whole carried 433,000 tons of cargo but by 1940 this was down to 151,000. In the now notorious LMS Act of 1944, the entire lengths of what today are known as the Montgomery and Llangollen Canals were

The Llangollen line has always been prone to breaches and has recently been subject to extensive (and expensive) renovations by British Waterways. This breach at Bryn Howell occurred in September 1960

British Waterways

abandoned. No commercial traffic had passed along the lines since 1939 and prospects of it returning in the face of rail and road competition were slight. Although the Montgomery line from Frankton was soon closed, in the event, the line from Hurleston to Llantisilio was kept, albeit only as a water channel to feed the Hurleston reservoir which supplies water to the taps of Crewe.

While this situation continued, the line deteriorated still further. In the summer of 1947, the canal was virtually impassable: Tom Rolt gave up trying to fight his way through the weed and dereliction and failed even to get as far as Chirk. By 1955, the official position (as defined by the Board of Survey to the British Transport Commission) was that there were no prospects of the canal generating enough commercial activity to justify its continued maintenance for navigation. Luckily, local enthusiasts, led by Trevor William, clerk of Wrexham Rural District Council, disagreed. They rallied support for the canal to be restored as a holiday route and their actions led to the reclassification of the line in 1968, when the Llangollen was recognized as a cruiseway under the Transport Act. Since then, and at great cost, the line has been gradually improved into the wonderful holiday route that it is today.

The Walk

Start:	Chirk (OS ref: SJ 291376) or Fron Cysyllte (OS ref: SJ 272413)
Finish:	Llangollen (OS ref: SJ 215422) or Horseshoe Falls (OS ref: SJ 195433)
Distance:	Minimum 5 miles/8 km Maximum 11 miles/18 km
Maps:	OS Landranger 117 (Chester), 125 (Bala & Lake Vrynwy) and 126 (Shrewsbury)
Outward:	Bryn Melyn buses from Market Street (Heol Y Farchnad), Llangollen, opposite central car park and public conveniences. Telephone: (0978) 860701. There are extra buses on Wednesdays and Saturdays but, sadly, none on Sundays
Return:	To Llangollen from Horeshoe Falls: Llangollen (steam) Railway from Berwyn station. Telephone: (0978) 860951
Car park:	Central car park in Llangollen
Public transport:	Chirk has a BR station

This excellent walk can be sub-divided to suit all needs. The full walk goes from Chirk to the end of the canal at Horseshoe Falls from where, if you arrive on

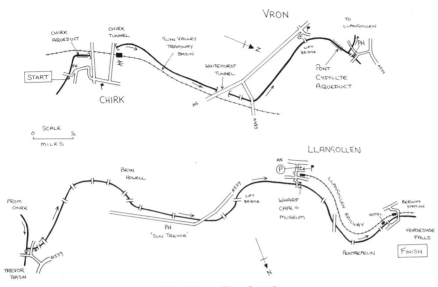

The Llangollen Canal

time, you can return to Llangollen by steam railway. If this proves impossible or undesirable, the walk can be halted 2 miles short at Llangollen Wharf. The start of the walk at Chirk is reached by bus from Llangollen. However, the stretch between Chirk and Fron Cysyllte (locally known as Vron) involves passing through two very dark and claustrophobic tunnels which some walkers may wish to avoid. If this is the case, I suggest that you take the bus only as far as Vron and walk from there, a distance of 5 miles to Llangollen.

Chirk to Fron Cysyllte

The bus from Llangollen stops in the centre of Chirk from where walkers should continue along the road signposted to Shrewsbury. This bends right down a hill and then swings around left. Cross the road to reach a footpath sign pointing over a stile to the right. This isn't the way of the walk but it is worth taking the path down into a field where there is a fine view of the Llangollen Canal's Chirk Aqueduct and the BR viaduct which is just beyond and above it.

Return to the road and continue on to 'the last pub in England', The Bridge. Take the small road (signposted to Weston Rhyn) that rises up by the pub to a post office and canal bridge. Turn right to take the towpath which is on the right-hand side of the canal.

After passing a house festooned with canal memorabilia, the line turns abruptly right to cross the 696 ft long Chirk Aqueduct. The aqueduct, although eclipsed in fame by its near neighbour at Pont Cysyllte, is nevertheless a splendid structure. Jessop, in proposing that the aqueduct be built, said 'instead of an obstruction it will be a romantic feature in the view'. And he was right. The contract for the work was let in January 1796 to William Hazeldine, John Simpson and William Davies but the design is Telford's. The aqueduct consists of a masonry structure within which is a canal bed made of iron plates bolted together. The plates are secured to the masonry sides in such a way that they tie the walls together to resist the lateral pressure of the water which could have led to blow-outs. The use of the cast-iron plates significantly reduced the weight of the structure (compared with masonry and clay puddling) and enabled the aqueduct to be built some 70 ft above the River Ceiriog below. It was finished in 1801 at a cost of £20,898. The railway viaduct, which carries the line from Shrewsbury to Chester (stopping at Chirk station), was built in the 1840s. What could have been a scenic disaster was happily avoided and the two structures complement each other splendidly to form a memorable spectacle.

Chirk Aqueduct and Viaduct

Half way across the aqueduct we return to Wales (is there any finer border crossing?) and from there we reach Chirk Tunnel. Opened in June 1802, the tunnel is unusual in having a towpath along its right-hand wall, a contribution to the development of canal tunnels made by Telford who plainly thought the practice of 'legging' to be rather old fashioned. Those who suffer even the remotest hint of claustrophobia should not attempt to go through the tunnel as the centre is pitch black and progress is only possible by going blindly onwards while clinging desperately on to the railings. Those with young children should certainly not attempt it as the railings do not require limbo dancing skills to pass under. Instead, take the path that goes up to the right of the tunnel entrance to a road which runs parallel with the tunnel and on to the railway station from where the towpath can be rejoined. For those who do walk through, it is a curious experience and one can only wonder what the horses made of the sudden plunge into darkness.

The tunnel opens into the fresh air and a cutting. For those who have followed Tom Rolt's progress along the Llangollen in *Landscape with Canals*, it was the collapse of this cutting which finally ended Rolt's attempt to reach Pont Cysyllte in 1947. The cutting leads shortly to a winding hole on the far bank. At one time here on the right was Black Park Basin, a canal-railway interchange where cargo was transhipped between the canal and the Glyn Valley tramway. This narrow gauge line was built to link with the slate and granite quarries in the Ceiriog Valley. Coal was also transhipped here from the local collieries. Sadly, the line was closed in 1935.

After the canal narrows (note the stop planks and slot designed to separate the section in the event of repair or breach), the line passes the newly built (June 1991) Chirk Marina with mooring spaces and a small shop (not accessible to towpathers). The line now passes through a second tunnel, the 191 yd long Whithurst Tunnel, which goes under Telford's later engineering venture, the Holyhead Road or A5. This tunnel, although much shorter and lighter than that at Chirk, should also be treated with caution by those with small children.

The canal now passes under two bridges to a point where it bends left. Here the Offa's Dyke long distance path joins the Llangollen Canal and the quality of the towpath improves somewhat. The canal enters a concrete-lined section as it follows the hillside on the south-western side of the Dee Valley. In this short stretch the line passes through a narrowed section with stop plank slots and then crosses a small aqueduct before reaching the site of an old quay. This huge site was formerly connected with the Pen-y-Craig limestone quarries. The large edifice which fronts the canal here contains a series of lime kilns which open out at canal level so that their product could be loaded directly on to boats for subsequent shipment. From here it is just a couple of hundred yards to the lift bridge (No. 28) which marks our arrival at Fron Cysyllte.

Fron Cysyllte to Llangollen

For those starting at Vron bus-stop, follow the advice of a signpost to the aqueduct (or Pont Cario Dwr) which points down the hill to the left. This soon reaches the aforementioned lift bridge. Cross the bridge and turn left.

From the lift bridge, the canal turns sharply right through a heavily wooded section which marks the start of the 97 ft high embankment built as the preliminary for the crossing of the Dee Valley. At the time of its construction, this was the highest man-made embankment in the country and was itself a significant achievement. But, as the wood thins, the staggering engineering

The pillars of Pont Cysyllte Aqueduct

prowess that was needed to span the Dee is evident as the ground suddenly falls away to reveal Pont Cysyllte (pronounced pont-kur-sulth-ter) Aqueduct, surely one of the greatest sights of the entire British canal network. Designed by Telford and Jessop and constructed by the ironmaster William Hazeldine, it took ten years to build and was finally opened on 26 November 1805. The aqueduct consists of 418 cast-iron plates bolted together to form a 1,007 ft long metal trough carried on nineteen stone piers across the valley. The design therefore differs from Chirk Aqueduct where only the bed was made of cast iron. Tom Rolt reports in *Landscape with Canals* that the plates used to make the trough were cast at Plas Kynaston on the site now occupied by the massive chemical works whose chimneys are to be seen on the other side of the Dee Valley at Trevor. The plates were then moved to the site by means of a temporary inclined tramway and assembled, rather precariously, *in situ*. Seemingly the opening of the aqueduct was greeted with great celebrations which included a salute from a cannon and various musical tributes from boatloads of floating bandsmen. The aqueduct cost a cool £47,018 (about £8,500 for the embankment, £17,300 for the iron work and £21,150 for the masonry). But wasn't it worth it!

The towpath across the aqueduct is cantilevered over the trough to provide a somewhat airy experience that may alarm those with no head for heights. There is, however, a strong handrail which can be clung to as the holiday-makers, coach parties, cyclists and joggers struggle to pass one another some 126 ft above the River Dee. But the structure is firm enough. The piers are standing on solid sandstone and were themselves made hollow towards the top in order to reduce their weight and save on masonry.

Pont Cysyllte is drained every eight years or so for maintenance by blocking off both ends with stop planks and then drawing a plug in the trough. The resulting cascade of water, which appears like a high free-falling waterfall, must be a somewhat alarming sight for those below who don't realize what precisely is going on.

At the far end a notice, in both English and Welsh, details the aqueduct's statistics. Almost immediately opposite, on the left-hand bank, a narrow channel heads off towards Llangollen, whereas a wide channel, in what is now Trevor Wharf, lies directly ahead. This is the only remaining remnant of the line that was originally intended to continue on to Chester and it runs for just a couple of hundred yards before coming to a stop at a former railway interchange basin. A number of boats moor at Trevor Wharf where there is a small canal shop, some public conveniences and the highly convenient Telford Inn.

Our route continues through the horse tunnel of the small road bridge and up right to the road. Here turn right to cross the bridge. From the bridge there is a good view of all that remains of Trevor Basin: two wharf arms that go either side of what was formerly the site of a railway terminus. Having abandoned the idea of a line to Chester, a short canal (of about a $\frac{1}{3}$ mile) called the Plas Kynaston

Canal was built to the Plas Kynaston iron foundry and factory, now the site of the chemical works over to the right. This ran from the right hand arm as seen from the bridge. The Plas Kynaston Canal closed in about 1914.

To continue the walk, go along the road to a T-junction. Turn left to pass the Telford Inn to another small bridge (which was being rebuilt when I passed) which goes over the canal. If you wish to get an excellent view of the aqueduct (best on a sunny late afternoon or early evening) continue down the road for a short distance when the view opens out to the left. If not, turn right at the bridge to take the right-hand bank. At the first bridge, the towpath changes sides.

This channel on from Trevor Wharf is notably narrower than the Llangollen Canal before Pont Cysyllte and was never intended to be a prime navigable route. Indeed the only reason it was built was to act as a feeder from the Dee at the Horseshoe Falls, some 2 miles beyond Llangollen at Llantisilio. An indication of its use can be seen by the strong current which flows from the direction of Llangollen, an unusual sight in an artificial waterway. This line along the Vale of Llangollen could have developed, however, as in 1801 there was a proposal for a line called the Merionethshire Canal which would have taken the canal on to Barmouth on the west Wales coast. If built, it would have been an important conduit for the many quarries and mines in that part of Wales.

Whether wide or narrow, the route between Trevor and Llangollen is a contour-hugging line high above the River Dee on the northern hillside. It must be one of the most delightful stretches of canal in the country: quiet, wooded and with magnificent views down to the Dee on the left. When looking at the terrain, it is remarkable that the entire length between Chirk and Llangollen is free of any locks. And yet this stretch has been a constant trial to British Waterways. The proof of this is seen after passing under three bridges (Nos. 33–5) and following the canal right to a point where the view to the left opens out. This stretch, near a BW noticeboard, has been breached three times since the 1950s: in 1960, 1982 and 1985. As a result, the entire length has been completely rebuilt with a reinforced-concrete trough overlying a specially developed high-drainage bed which hopefully should prevent any further movement of the underlying hillside. In fact, the whole line between Chirk and Llangollen is gradually being upgraded by BW at a cost of over five million pounds. Such, albeit expensive, rebuilding should hopefully keep this superb waterway open into the forseeable future but one can guess what the response of the authorities would have been had these slips occurred before the Second World War rather than after it. Surely a simple pipe would have been easier and cheaper, and we can only be grateful that one was never installed.

The line continues under bridges 36 and 37 to reach a rather angular winding hole, a sizeable hotel and bridge 38 (Bryn Howell Bridge). Bridge 39 is an old concrete affair which formerly carried the Llangollen Railway to Ruabon and, who knows, may do so again some day. Just before bridge 40 stands a 2 ft high concrete roofed shed which holds the stop planks which are used to slide down the slot near the bridge itself. Shortly thereafter, the canal is joined by the A539 Trevor to Llangollen road which runs close to the right bank for nearly 1 mile and past the Sun Trevor pub.

Sun Trevor Bridge (No. 41) marks the site of one of the first breaches in the post-war series. In 1945, the bank here slipped and washed down to the railway below, taking a hapless goods train with it. The engine driver was killed. Another collapse occurred a little further on in 1947, luckily with less serious results. However, the subsequent loss of water reduced levels throughout the length of the canal and nearly prevented Tom Rolt from escaping to the Shropshire Union main line after his aborted journey in 1947. Such unhappy memories should not, however, mar the superb views to the left across the Dee Valley to Llangollen which can now be seen in the distance approximately $1\frac{1}{2}$ miles away.

The stretch between bridges 41 and 42 is incredibly narrow and portends things to come. There are just three possible passing places in a $\frac{1}{3}$ mile, as the canal struggles to find a way between the precipitous drop to the left and the hard-faced rocks to the right. If you're lucky enough to be here at a time when it isn't pouring with rain (the author wasn't), the next stretch offers a delightful mixture of pastoral, mountainous and watery scenes. Just after the lift bridge (No. 44), the canal is forced against some sheer cliff faces overhung by trees before finally winding its way through the outskirts of Llangollen. Again the line narrows so that there is only room for one boat at a time. Navigation guides suggest 'tact and restraint' to boat captains although from the look of it not all have read the right books. To the left, below the towpath, the bank drops sharply to the road below. Soon, through the trees to the left, the outskirts of Llangollen appear. After a while the canal widens and is lined with moored boats as we come out from under the trees to enter the town.

We soon reach Llangollen Wharf which is positioned high above the town, with a fine view down to the river and the main street. The wharf building has been converted into a café and a small canal museum at one end, and into stabling at the other. On appropriate days, the occupants of the stables can be seen plying their trade with boatloads of, not always cheerful-looking, holiday-makers being towed upstream towards the Horseshoe Falls in horse-drawn barges.

There are now some 2 miles to the origin of the Llangollen Canal. If you wish to check on the availability of a steam train return, take the paths either to the left or right of the wharf building that go down to Abbey Road from where the Llangollen Railway station is easily spotted. If you've decided to stop here, Market Street can be found by crossing the Dee Bridge and following the parking and public convenience signs.

Llangollen to Llantisilio

This final section of the walk could also make a fine afternoon stroll in its own right. From the wharf (well signposted from Abbey Road), turn left to pass along the tree-lined canal. Touring boats visiting Llangollen are only able to go about 50 yd beyond the wharf, where there is the last winding hole that could allow them to turn. However, the towpath continues through the outskirts of the town and past the famous International Eisteddfod ground, which is on the left-hand side before bridge 46. Train line and canal then follow each other around the contours to reach Pentrefelin, now the site of a motor museum. From 1852, this was a wharf from where a tramway went $4\frac{1}{2}$ miles up the Horseshoe Pass (to the right) to the slate quarries at Oernant and Moel y Faen.

Eventually the path runs round to reach the Chain Bridge Hotel. From here the intrepid towpather ignores a rather begrudging Shropshire Union notice and goes on under a pleasant stone road bridge (Kings Bridge) to a small hut built by the water authorities in 1947 to control the flow of water into the canal. Six million gallons per day flow into the line which starts here. Beyond the hut a path leads into a field and to the Horseshoe Falls, an arc-shaped weir built by Telford to supply water to the canal.

To reach the railway station return back under Kings Bridge to the hotel where there is a metal footbridge which goes over the canal and up the cliff to a road. Turn left to go round and over the road bridge. This eventually reaches Berwyn station from where trains can be caught into Llangollen.

Further Explorations

Comparatively close to Chirk and Llangollen is the Montgomery Canal, currently the scene of much excitement and activity as enthusiasts strive to restore it to its former glory.

The Montgomeryshire Canal Act was passed in 1794 and took a line from the Ellesmere Canal at Llanymynech to Welshpool and Newtown. Later the stretch from the Llangollen at Frankton also became known as the Montgomery Canal and this means that the waterway today follows a total of 35 miles. Sadly, following a serious breach in 1936, the London, Midland & Scottish Railway, who then owned the line, successfully had the canal abandoned by an Act of 1944. It quickly decayed and would undoubtedly have disappeared from the landscape had not a group of enthusiasts started to restore the line in 1969. By

1987, an Act of Parliament was passed which should enable full restoration of what Charles Hadfield considers to be Britain's loveliest canal.

Although it is possible to walk most of the 35 miles to Newtown, a flavour of the Montgomery can be had with a brief walk and a couple of visits. The line starts at the Frankton Junction with the Llangollen. This can be found by taking the A495 which runs between Oswestry and Ellesmere/Whitchurch. At the village of Welsh Frankton, a signpost points south to Lower Frankton. This small road twists and turns around a series of farms eventually to reach a canal bridge (over the Llangollen Canal) and some verge side parking. For a walk of about 1 mile, go back to the bridge and turn right through a gate. After about 20 to 30 yd, you will reach Frankton Junction. If you turn right here you will shortly come to the first locks on the Montgomery Canal, a staircase of two – where the bottom gate of the first is the top gate of the second. Some of the original buildings still line the canal, although none perform their original task of toll-house, keeper's cottage or inn. Two further locks, restored in 1987, are passed before this short stretch comes to an end and the weeds take over. Continue along the clear footpath which runs to the right of the line to a point where a reed-ridden basin is reached near a small, but high, road bridge (Lockgate Bridge). To the left, a straight line of plant growth can be traced running off to the east. This is the former Weston branch which went on for 5 miles to Weston Lullingfields. It seems impossible to believe that this would have been part of the main-line route from Chester to Shrewsbury had the original Ellesmere Canal plan been carried out. To return to the car, you can either retrace your steps or go up by the side of the bridge to the road. By turning right, you can then follow the lane back to the parking space.

From Llanymynech, the line can be followed south to the newly (1986) restored Carreghofa Locks and then on to Vrynwy Aqueduct. Some 6 miles of waterway are also open for use around Welshpool.

Further Information

The Llangollen and Montgomery Canals are both part of the old Shropshire Union and are ably served by:

The Shropshire Union Canal Society Ltd,
Mrs Mary Awcock,
'Oak Haven',
Longden-on-Tern,
Telford,
TF6 6LJ.

The society's immediate aim is to reopen the Montgomery Canal and members are actively involved in this work. Should you wish to become involved in any capacity then new members are very welcome.

The history of the canal can be traced through:
Hadfield, Charles, *The Canals of the West Midlands*. David & Charles, 1969.

If you are interested in following the entire line:
Pellow,T. and Bowen, P., *Canal to Llangollen*. Landscape Press, 1988.

The trials and tribulations of trying to reach Llangollen in the late 1940s can be followed in:
Rolt, L.T.C., *Landscape with Canals*. Alan Sutton Publishing, 1977.

8
THE NORTH WALSHAM & DILHAM CANAL

Honing to Tonnage Bridge

Introduction

For those who find the industrial nature of the British canal system a bit grating, the North Walsham & Dilham is heaven sent. A neglected line, way out on a limb on the northern fringe of the Norfolk Broads, the NW & D is more of a nature reserve than a commercial waterway and my guess is that it will probably stay that way. There are no boats on the NW & D nor, in some places, any water. But perhaps most strangely, in these days when virtually anything that's derelict has somebody trying to breathe life back into it, it doesn't have a restoration society either. Or have I spoke too soon?

The North Walsham & Dilham Canal is on the northernmost fringes of the Norfolk Broads. From Barton Broad (a couple of miles north-east of Wroxham), the River Ant can be traced north and west, away from the town of Stalham to Wayford Bridge, a point about 1 mile east of the village of Dilham. Here the $8\frac{3}{4}$ mile long North Walsham & Dilham Canal starts life by taking a course that runs north and then west to reach the small village of Honing. At Briggate, the line returns to a more northerly course to skirt around the eastern fringes of North Walsham towards Ebridge, Bacton Wood and Swafield. From there, the canal formerly ran a short distance to its terminus in a basin adjacent to Antingham Mills. Antingham Ponds, to the north-west of the basin, was the ultimate limit of navigation but primarily acted as a reservoir and feeder to the canal line.

There's only sporadic industrial archaeology interest along the NW & D but it makes for a fine place to spend a warm, sunny afternoon among the butterflies, dragonflies, herons and sparrow-hawks. If you're more used to the glories of the Walsall Canal, you just might come here to see how the other half live.

History

In 1810, the River Ant was already navigable from the northern Norfolk Broads to the small hamlet of Dilham where a thriving local trade took goods and produce to and from the villages further north. Corn and flour from the mills around North Walsham and Antingham were shipped from Dilham to Yarmouth and commodities such as coal, marl and oilcake were imported via the Dilham staithes or wharves. With the success of the many canals around the country, it must have only been a matter of time before suggestions were made to extend the Ant artificially towards the town of North Walsham and, during the course of 1811, no fewer than three plans for a new navigation were widely circulated. The first was a scheme by William Youard and there were two by John Millington of Hammersmith. Interest was such that a meeting was held on 14 September at the King's Arms in North Walsham where it was immediately decided to petition Parliament for an Act to make 'a cut or canal for boats from the River Ant . . . at or near a place called Wayford Bridge near Dilham to the towns of North Walsham and Antingham'.

The bill was read on 18 February 1812 and despite opposition from the inhabitants of Dilham and Worstead, who feared loss of their wharf and carrying businesses, the Act received royal assent on 5 May 1812. The Act authorized the raising of £33,000 plus a further £10,000 by mortgage of the rates and dues if the original sum wasn't enough. The Act also authorized tolls of 1d. per mile for passengers, $\frac{1}{2}$d. per mile for cattle, horses and asses, and 6d. a score for sheep and pigs.

Despite the initial enthusiasm and the fact that the share issue was virtually fully subscribed, the final authority to start the construction work was not given until 15 December 1824. During the period of inactivity, the proprietors had spent some time fighting off claims for damages from those who feared loss of trade due to the new line. Digging, in fact, finally began on 5 April 1825 with a crew of some one hundred navvies from Bedfordshire under the control of the engineer John Millington and the clerk to the committee, William Youard. The first day of digging was one of great celebration with the navvies parading in the market place of North Walsham. With the committee and a band before them, they then marched off to Austin Bridge, where the first sod was cut by William Youard and the band played 'God Save the King'. The work for the day stopped shortly thereafter and everybody went back to the market 'to partake of some barrels of strong beer'.

Curiously, the NW & D was John Millington's only venture into canal engineering and he later emigrated to America, where he apparently used his enormous experience to write books on the subject. It must also be said that actual day-to-day supervision of the works wasn't carried out by Millington at

By the turn of the twentieth century, the canal had little or no traffic and maintenance levels were declining. Honing Lock, here photographed in the 1920s, remained operational until about 1935 but has since been converted into a weir and, as towpathers will have noticed, has become considerably overgrown

Norfolk County Council

all but by a contractor, Thomas Hughes, who officially succeeded Millington as engineer in 1827. Hughes was actually a much more experienced civil engineer having worked on the Caledonian, Dingwall and Edinburgh & Glasgow Union Canals, as well as on various harbour and river works.

Although there were few significant construction works along the line, the land through which the canal passes is very boggy in places and Hughes had some problems in establishing a firm line through the peat and in building embankments. Despite this, he had completed enough to allow the first laden wherries to reach Cubitt's Mill on 14 June 1826. In what seems to have been typical reaction throughout the construction of the line thousands of spectators were reported to have assembled to witness this interesting scene with the day finishing with a treat for the workmen of Mr Sharpe's strong ale and Barclay's brown stout. The official opening of the completed line took place not long after on 29 August 1826. This time there was a flotilla of boats that spent the day going up and down the $8\frac{3}{4}$ miles of the canal, no doubt with the consumption of yet more strong ale. The final cost of the new line was approximately £29,300, one of the few canals that was actually built to estimate. Hughes needed six locks, built at Honing, Briggate, Ebridge, Bacton Wood and two at Swafield to take the canal up 58 ft from Wayford Bridge to Antingham.

Conventional narrowboats were never used on the NW & D. Instead, a type of small Norfolk wherry of about 18 to 20 tons and measuring 50 ft long by 12 ft 4 in beam with 3 ft draught was the norm. There was also, for example, one small 12 ton wherry, the *Cabbage Wherry*, which regularly ran vegetables from Antingham to Yarmouth. In addition because of the shallowness of the canal, there were some vessels of a type known as slip-keel wherries in which the keel could be unbolted and removed when the craft was about to enter shallow water.

The NW & D was primarily used to ship corn, flour, mill offals, feed cake, manure and wood. Interestingly although some coal traffic went along the line, it still proved to be cheaper to drop coal from the collieries of north-eastern England on to the beaches of the Norfolk coast at Mundesley or Bacton, and then to transport it overland in carts. The canal's share of the coal traffic was further limited later by the introduction of the railway which ran from Norwich to Cromer.

In common with many other canals whose prosperity relied primarily on shipping agricultural produce, the NW & D was never a financial success. Even as early as 1830, the price of a £50 share had dropped to £10 and there seemed to be little prospect of increasing trade. In 1866 the proprietors gained powers (from an Act) to let them sell the canal. In fact, nothing happened until 17 December 1885 when the company clerk, James Turner, informed the Board of Trade that the Bacton Wood miller and wherry owner, Edward Press, was buying the line. The deal, worth just £600, was completed on 16 March 1886.

It was required by the 1866 Act that the sum received from the sale be divided among the known shareholders in proportion to their holdings in the company. James Turner was entrusted with the task but after paying out just a few of the shareholders he absconded with the balance which was never seen again. The canal committee thought themselves to be morally if not legally bound to reimburse the money and, in 1896, each of the five proprietors, including Edward Press, donated nearly £111 to make up the sum necessary for the payments.

During the course of 1887, further problems within the operation of the company were spotted by Walter Rye, a solicitor who had become principal clerk. There had been 'great irregularites in the management and direction of the Company . . . amounting to an almost total disregard to the provisions of the Act'. The Act, for example, did not allow anybody holding a place of profit to serve on the committee but Edward Press had done so and, although a treasurer should have been appointed and security given by him, no such appointment had been made. Mr Rye also pointed out that there was no way of formally winding up the company without both huge expense and revealing the many irregularities. Interestingly, although these were fairly serious concerns, they appear to have been quietly forgotten about.

Meanwhile, traffic on the NW & D continued although the roughly $1\frac{1}{2}$ miles between Swafield and Antingham were abandoned in 1893. In 1898, 400 tons of local traffic, 5,000 tons of exports and 6,386 tons of imports were moved along the line. But by 1906 receipts were under £400 p.a. and, on 2 July of that year, Edward Press died. Although trade appeared to be in terminal decline, the canal was sold by auction on 11 September 1907 to a Mr Percy, a director of the General Estates Company, for £2,550. The company already owned the rights of the Gorleston ferry and of the tolls of Selby Bridge and were associated with the Yarmouth & Gorleston Steamboat Company. They didn't keep the canal for long. In 1921, the canal was taken over by E.G. Cubitt and G. Walker (for £1,500) who then promptly sold it to a newly formed company, the North Walsham Canal Company Ltd.

The canal itself was, by now, in a poor state of repair. It had been badly

Honing Lock, 1991

damaged in floods in August 1912 when a bank was breached above Bacton Wood Lock. Attempts were made during the 1920s to improve the canal below Swafield but there was little or no improvement in traffic and the section from Antingham to Swafield Bridge was closed in 1927 by warrant of the Ministry of Transport. The last commercial boat on the canal was the wherry *Ella*, owned by the descendants of Edward Press, which loaded cargo at Bacton Wood Staithe in December 1934. Soon after this the canal became heavily silted and eventually derelict. The bottom three locks were in use until 1935 but there appears to be no record of them being used subsequently.

The only section that is even vaguely navigable today is the stretch from Wayford Bridge to the tail of Honing Lock and large stretches above that are dry. Interestingly, the canal wasn't nationalized and it remains, at least nominally, in the ownership of the North Walsham Canal Company.

The Walk

Start and finish:	Weaver's Way car park, Station Road, Honing (the old Honing railway station (OS ref: TG 317276)
Distance:	5¼ miles/8¼ km
Map:	OS Landranger 133 (North East Norfolk)
Car Park:	As above
Public transport:	None. The closest public transport gets is North Walsham which is on the BR line from Norwich to Cromer. As the Weaver's Way passes through North Walsham, it is possible to start the walk from there by following the course of this reasonably well signposted long-distance path. A return walk will, however, add an extra 8½ miles to the distance

To reach the Weaver's Way car park leave the main A149 (North Walsham to Stalham road) near Lyngate where there is a signpost towards Honing. After about a ½ mile, the road goes over the canal at Briggate. It's worth a quick stop here to see the surprisingly well-preserved remains of Briggate Lock which are right next to the bridge. Continue along the road towards Honing for another 250 yd to a point where a signpost indicates left for the Weaver's Way car park. This was formerly the car park of Honing railway station that has been sequestered by Norfolk County Council for users of the long-distance path. The Weaver's Way, opened in 1980 and so-called to commemorate the former local industry, originally ran for 15 miles between Blickling Hall and Stalham. Since then, various bits have been added and you can now walk a total of 56 miles from Cromer to Great Yarmouth. Should you wish to do so that is.

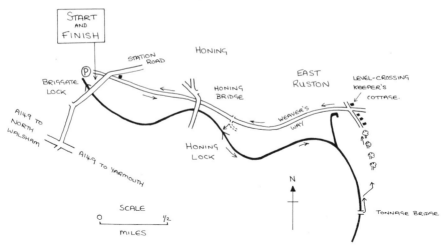

The North Walsham & Dilham Canal

The walk starts by circumnavigating the station platform to arrive down at railway track level and then turning right. The Weaver's Way uses the track of the former Midland & Great Northern Joint Railway (the M & GNJR), a line that went from North Walsham to Great Yarmouth which was closed in February 1959. Most of the line has been converted to road and, if one looks at a map, it seems amazing that this bit survived untarmacked. The clear, if somewhat overgrown, track leads immediately to a gate to cross Station Road, through another gate and back on to the line. Just by the second gate is a level-crossing keeper's cottage, now a private house.

The railway path leads through open country to reach a crossroad where the promisingly named Canal Farm Lane leads right to Canal Farm. We, meanwhile, continue along the railway with views to Honing to the left. Within a couple of hundred yards, the route enters woodland. The path remains clear and is bordered on either side by an almost hidden railway boundary fence. This soon reaches the rather fine iron Honing Road Bridge. Just before the bridge on the right is the site of the former Honing Wharf or Staithe. A short 110 yd long cut was made from the main line to the wharf so that cargo could be unloaded as near to the village as possible. After the bridge, the main course of the North Walsham & Dilham Canal joins the track to the right. The canal which is heavily overgrown with reeds then turns right while the railway path continues past a house to reach another crossroad track. Turn right here and, following a footpath sign, immediately right again to take a narrow path over a small ditch to a bigger bridge which crosses the canal at the site of an old lock. Honing Lock is now nothing more than a weir but still bears the long redundant winding gear

Briggate Lock on the North Walsham & Dilham Canal

and high lock walls. Honing was the first lock (of a total of six) on the canal from the River Ant at Wayford Bridge.

Cross the bridge and turn left to follow a clear path that gives the impression of moving away from the canal. It doesn't. Within 10 to 20 yd, the path arrives on the right-hand bank of the line that is now passing through dense woodland. Shortly, the path goes through a gate to reach an open field. This stretch of the canal sports the finest growth of yellow water-lilies outside of a stately home.

The canal continues around a large arc for the next 2 miles. At one point a short branch (of just under a $\frac{1}{2}$ mile) runs off to the north from the left-hand bank in the direction of East Ruston but other than that the canal and the country are quiet, relaxing and in perfect harmony. It is an excellent linear wildlife park and towpathers can only be grateful that the Anglian Water Authority (as it then was) stopped pumping effluent into the canal in 1980. It's not until the towpath is pushed away from the canal by a dense hedge near Oaks Farm that the mind is forced back into action and some thought processes are required once again.

A gap in the hedge leads to a lane. Turn left to reach Tonnage Bridge. When the canal was in use, there was a small wharf and a cottage here and the bridge was used as a convenient spot to monitor the flow of traffic along the line and to levy tolls on goods entering and leaving the canal. The cottage and wharf have now disappeared and so did the bridge, nearly. It was restored in 1982 by the local landowner in the same style as the original, if marginally wider. A noticeboard, put up by the Broads Authority, explains the history of the bridge and, usefully, provides a map for the next section of the walk.

Cross the bridge and turn left to go over a stile. Keep near the canal until the next stile where a brook going off to the right is marked by a row of small trees. Take a diagonal course across this field (and away from the canal) to a gate. Cross the stile here and walk on for nearly a $\frac{1}{2}$ mile, crossing another stile, to reach a gate. This goes into an unmetalled lane past a small number of houses to reach a five-bar gate and the Weaver's Way. This is another old level-crossing and the keeper's cottage is to the right. Turn left to walk along the railway path. Within a short distance, an expanse of water to the left marks the terminus of the East Garston branch of the canal.

Peace and solitude near Tonnage Bridge

Keep on the Weaver's Way path which will take you back under Honing Bridge to the car park at Honing railway station.

Further Explorations

Unlike most of the canals in this book, the NW & D is not under the stewardship of British Waterways and thus there is no broad-brush permission to walk along the towpath of the canal. Walkers must stay on public rights of way where available and it has to be said that few are. Regrettably, therefore, it is not possible to walk the entire length of the NW & D nor even to visit some of the more interesting features. We can only peer across fields or over bridges in the hope of being able to follow the line or identify the remains of the occasional lock.

The ultimate end of the canal at Antingham Ponds can be explored by a short stroll of about 2 miles around the virtually traffic-free lanes north of North Walsham. The walk starts at Lyngate (OS ref: TG 275316 on map 133).

From North Walsham, take the Mundesley Road (B1145) which runs north-east from the A149. After about a $\frac{1}{2}$ mile, a signpost indicates Lyngate (not to be confused with the Lyngate near Honing). Follow this lane until you meet a road which comes in from the left. Park on a verge near here. Continue along the road and turn right. After about a $\frac{1}{4}$ mile, the lane goes over a former canal bridge. Antingham Basin is to the left and the final locks at Swafield are away to the right. The lane shortly turns sharp left and continues past a turning to Bradfield to reach a now closed-off turning to the left. This was formerly the entrance to the Antingham bone mills and the canal terminus basin which were both in the field over to the left. The lane continues round to a point where a road comes in from the left. Continue straight on for a short distance and look left to see Antingham Ponds, the feeder reservoir for the canal. Return to the junction and turn right. This lane crosses two bridges over streams. Both were formerly navigable although only by small lighters. If you turn left at the next turning, you will shortly arrive back at Lyngate.

Further Information

There is little or no information on the NW&D and it would seem to be a good area for some fresh research. Most of the information included here came from: Boyes, J. and Russel, R., *The Canals of Eastern England*. David & Charles, 1977.

9
THE STAFFORDSHIRE & WORCESTERSHIRE CANAL

Stourport to Kidderminster

Introduction

The Staffordshire & Worcestershire Canal, or the Stour Cut as it became known to many of the boatman who worked it, was a true model for canal builders everywhere. As part of Brindley's grand plan to join the four corners of the country, it was one of the earliest canals built and yet it must rank among the very best. Undoubtedly the fact that it ran along such a vital route was important but the positive approach to its planning and execution must have helped. The proprietors knew precisely what they wanted and why. The S & W was efficiently built at a cost that was barely different from the budget. It immediately attracted a large amount of cargo and it yielded high and continuous dividends for over a century. All this and good looks too! It's the sort of thing that would make a mere mortal canal silt up with envy.

The S & W starts at a junction with the Trent & Mersey Canal at Great Haywood, a village about 5 miles east of Stafford. From here the canal widens to form Tixall Wide, a mini-Norfolk Broad on the outskirts of Cannock Chase. After Milford, the line goes under the M6 to reach Penkridge from where it continues south, twisting and turning along a typical Brindley contour-following line to Hatherton Junction. Here is the former Hatherton branch to the Birmingham Canal Navigations. After squeezing through a narrow sand-stone cutting, known as the Pendeford Rockin', the S & W reaches the outskirts of Wolverhampton. Here are two important junctions just a $\frac{1}{2}$ mile apart. First is the Autherley Junction with the Shropshire Union and then Aldersley Junction with the Birmingham Canal Navigations.

The course now passes Tettenhall and Compton to Wombourn where the locks and bridges around Bratch are a constant source of interest. After more tortuous bends, the S & W meets the Stourbridge Canal, another important route into central Birmingham. South of Stourton, the sandstone rocks force the canal into some amazing contortions: at Austcliff, near Cookley, a cliff overhangs the waterway; at Debdale, the lock seems to be built out of solid rock; a little further on the canal almost doubles back on itself. After all this excitement, it comes as a relief to reach the town of Kidderminster with its interesting array of canal-side buildings. After more fun with sandstone at Caldwall Lock, the line passes under the arches of the renascent Severn Valley Railway to continue gently down to Stourport, a town whose existence is solely due to Brindley's decision to join the River Severn there. Here are a marvellous collection of basins and buildings that would make a fine end for any canal.

There is no doubt that people seem to develop a deep and lasting affection for the S & W. It is a much loved canal and, consequently, one of the busiest.

History

Although Josiah Wedgwood and his colleagues saw the advantage of joining their proposed Trent & Mersey Canal with the River Severn, the decisive meeting at Wolseley Bridge in December 1765 concluded that the venture would be best left to others. So it was that a group led by James Perry met in Wolverhampton on 20 January 1766. By 19 March, they had decided to go ahead with the plan and authorized Hugh Henshall (James Brindley's brother-in-law) and Samuel Simcock to carry out a preliminary survey.

On 14 May 1766, the Act for a canal from the Trent & Mersey at Great Haywood to the River Severn at Little Mitton (now Stourport) was passed. It was to cost £70,000 (with £30,000 more if needed) and many local dignitaries chipped in. Earl Gower of Trentham, who had been a major player in the construction of the Trent & Mersey Canal, headed a list of the rich and famous which included Thomas Anson of Shugborough (whose land the northern end of the canal passed through), members of the Molineux family, the Earl of Stamford, Sir Richard Wrottesley and Sir Edward Littleton. The star canal builder of the age, James Brindley, was appointed surveyor and, with Perry as treasurer, building began. In fact, although Brindley laid out the line, the presumably grossly overworked maestro left the supervision of the engineering to Samuel Simcock and Thomas Dadford.

The construction of the S & W appears to have been both swift and efficient despite the fact that Brindley had not actually built locks before (the first is said to have been at Compton). By November 1770, following a supplementary Act to raise a mere £10,000, the canal was open from Stourport to Compton, near Wolverhampton (about 2¼ miles south of Aldersley Junction), and cargo from the Severn was already finding its way into the Midlands. The basin at Stourport

An early engraving by James Sheriff of the Stourport Basin as seen from the opposite bank of the River Severn. The Tontine Hotel can clearly be identified on the right, while the entrance to the canal can be seen in the top left-hand corner of the basin

British Waterways

was finished in 1771 and the whole line open for traffic on 28 May 1772 at a cost of about £100,000. The 46 miles of canal contained twelve locks from Great Haywood to the summit at Gailey and then thirty-one down from Compton to Stourport. Apart from two barge locks into the Severn, the canal was built to the Midlands narrowboat width of 7 ft. To add a further string to its bow, shortly after completion, on 21 September 1772, a line to central Birmingham became available when the Birmingham Canal was opened from the junction at Aldersley. It was thus now possible to navigate all the way from Bristol to central Birmingham for the first time.

The Staffordshire & Worcestershire Canal was a success from the beginning. Only eighteen months after opening, it was fully able to pay off its interest and provide its shareholders with a dividend of £4 a share. By 1775 the dividend had increased to £12. It is no wonder that, in 1783, £100 shares were trading for £400.

Further increases in trade followed the opening of the Dudley and Stourbridge Canals in 1779. Business at Stourport was such that it was rapidly becoming a major port for Staffordshire coal and all manner of manufactured goods such as ironware, glass, pottery and textiles from Birmingham, the Potteries and Manchester – much going to Bristol for export. In return, imports from Bristol and agricultural goods as well as cargo from the Coalbrookdale area were landed at Stourport on its way north. The affect that all this had on the previously insignificant spot now called Stourport was dramatic. The canal company built the basins and warehouses but there was a concomitant growth in houses, inns and various forms of industry, such as vinegar works, tan-yards, iron foundries and spinning mills.

The canal company was keen to build on this success and took efforts to promote connecting navigations. It actively supported the Stroudwater Navigation (from Framilode below Gloucester to Stroud) for example, and many of the personalities from the S & W subscribed to the Thames & Severn Canal which opened in 1789. This latter venture offered the potential of a somewhat lengthy line of $269\frac{1}{2}$ miles from London to Birmingham. This was a very short-lived hope as the Oxford Canal, opened in the same year as the Thames & Severn, reduced the distance to 227 miles and by 1805 the Grand Junction shortened it even more.

The main object of the S & W company's concern, however, was the River Severn. In 1784, it commissioned William Jessop to try to sort out problems with low water in summer months as well as to improve the towpaths. Although proposals on how to improve the river were forthcoming, the necessary powers to do so were not. Strong opposition came from those who now saw the opportunity for a more direct line between Worcester and Stourbridge. A second attempt to make improvements in 1790–1 similarly came to nought even though the necessary powers and funds were available. The situation came to a head with the proposal for the Worcester & Birmingham Canal which threatened to avoid the tricky bits of the Severn altogether and to take a large amount of the central Birmingham traffic. The S & W fought the proposal hard and initially had some success in defeating the bill of 1790. But with the passage of the 1791 Act, the W & B emerged as a potential threat to S & W business.

Despite this challenge, the following years further demonstrated the basic soundness of the S & W. A branch to Stafford along the Rivers Penk and Sow was opened to Radford Wharf in February 1816 and trade on the S & W continued to be good. In the years around 1815 the average annual dividend was £43 16s. With the completion of the Worcester & Birmingham in December 1815, much of the coal and other cargoes were permanently lost but the underlying strength of the company's trade meant that toll receipts were comparatively unaffected. Dividends fell initially to £33 a share but rose again to £40 p.a. within three years.

Although the current storm had been weathered, the forecast remained unpromising. More and more competition was coming from an ever improving transport network. In 1825, for example, Pickfords were advertising a road 'conveyance' between Kidderminster and Birmingham in direct competition with the S & W. In response, canal hours were extended with some boats being allowed to work overnight for the first time. By March 1830, the S & W had to follow the Birmingham canals in allowing all boats to work locks through the

Canal boats unloading coal on to a (rather posed) series of Baggeridge's carts at Kidderminster Wharf in the 1920s with St Mary and All Saints Church in the background. On the far left is a steam dredger

British Waterways, The Boat Museum archive

night. Nightmen were employed and lock-keepers paid extra for their night-time labours. Another consequence of increased competition was the intro-duction of a complex toll policy designed to encourage particular cargoes on particular routes to particular places. The discounts became ever more complic-ated and unpredictable and led to a series of complaints from short-distance carriers who often had to pay more than those going further.

The building of the Birmingham & Liverpool Junction Canal (B & LJ) was also to be a threat to the fortunes of the S & W. The B & LJ, now part of the Shropshire Union, ran from Autherley Junction to the Chester Canal at Nantwich. Shippers from Birmingham went along the Birmingham Canal to Aldersley, then along a $\frac{1}{2}$ mile of the S & W to Autherley and into the B & LJ. This line threatened the S & W's traffic from Autherley to the Trent & Mersey at Great Haywood and there was also concern that precious water would be lost down the new canal. Following their vigorous complaints, the S & W agreed to accept compensation for every lockful of water that flowed into the B & LJ. However, when the S & W ran short, permission was withdrawn and the B & LJ had to buy extra supplies from the Wyrley & Essington Canal (the northernmost of the Birmingham Canal Navigations). By the time the B & LJ opened on 2 March 1835, their promoters and users were growing rather tired of the S & W's high tolls and the pedantic fuss over water supplies. They decided to go over the S & W's heads. The plan was to build a mile long aqueduct 'fly-over' from the Birmingham Canal to the B & LJ; it would bypass the S & W altogether. The S & W were so shaken that they promptly agreed to reduce their tolls. So successful a trump card was this, that it was used twice more on different issues with similar effect in 1842 and 1867.

Throughout all these skirmishes, the S & W remained a solid, profitable company, further demonstrating that it was the right canal in the right place at the right time. In 1838, it carried 680,479 tons of goods and paid a £38 dividend on a £140 share. With such profits, the S & W was able to fund the Hatherton branch. This ran from Hatherton Junction about $5\frac{1}{2}$ miles north of Autherley to Churchbridge and was an important route for the collieries near Wyrley. The branch was further extended in 1863 to join the Wyrley & Essington Canal (part of the Birmingham Canal Navigations).

Following the first rumblings of railway competition in 1830, the S & W maintained a fiercely anti-railway stance and almost succeeded in forming an anti-train alliance with the other canal companies of the region. It was vigorous in its condemnation of schemes to convert canals to railways and insisted that the closure of any one canal was a blow to all canals. But such forthright resolution cracked in 1847. Perhaps the damage to the waterways network had already been done by then but there was a dramatic U-turn and the company declared that it would welcome an amalgamation with a railway company in order to guarantee continuing dividends. In the event, the company didn't succeed in this and it didn't really need to. Toll receipts remained high and 14 per cent dividends continued into the 1870s. Various schemes were devised to modernize the line and to expand its influence. It formed its own carrying company, became part of the trust to work the Thames & Severn Canal, and bought the Severn Towpath Company. But all these ventures were fighting the inevitable. Although the canal was still carrying some 722,000 tons of cargo in 1905, the best days were clearly over.

The story of the first half of the twentieth century is one of gradually declining trade and influence. Remarkably, however, the company was still independent and still able to pay $2\frac{1}{2}$ per cent dividends right up to the time when it was nationalized in 1948, a situation that was mostly thanks to a continuing coal trade. But the gradual incursion of the railways and the improvement of the roads eventually had their effect. The last regular commercial traffic was the carriage of Cannock Chase coal to Stourport power station. This business, which apparently involved some seventy pairs of narrow boats, came to an end in the 1950s.

The Report of the Board of Survey to the British Transport Commission had mixed feelings about the S & W. It concluded that there was no need to retain

both it and the Worcester & Birmingham Canal, which in its view formed
alternative routes from the Severn to the Midlands. In 1959, the Bowes
Committee of Inquiry recommended that the S & W be closed. This bureau-
cratic decision, which mirrored the prevailing view about the country's
waterways at that time, prompted action from local canal supporters. The S &
W Canal Society was formed in the same year with the aim of developing and
maintaining the line. Luckily for us, the wolves were held off long enough by
both the society and the Inland Waterways Association to take the canal
network into a more sympathetic age. In the Transport Act of 1968, both the
Worcester & Birmingham and the entire length of the S & W were declared a
cruiseway and British Waterways were given the authority to maintain them to a
navigable standard. The future of the S & W was thus assured. Today, the line
is not only open but full of vigour and a much-loved cruising route through the
west Midlands.

The Walk

Start:	At Stourport Basin (OS ref: SO 810710)
Finish:	Kidderminster Lock (OS ref: SO 829768)
Distance:	4¾ miles/7 km
Map:	OS Landranger 138 (Kidderminster & Wyre Forest Area)
Return:	Midland Red West Buses 11–16. Very regular, even on Sundays. Leave from Town Hall, Kidderminster to Stourport Basin (York Street). Telephone: (0562) 823631
Car park:	At Severn Bridge, Stourport or signposted multi-storey in central Kidderminster
Public transport:	Kidderminster has a BR main-line station which runs to Birmingham New Street

The walk starts at Stourport and goes to Kidderminster but could equally easily
go the other way. I chose to park in Kidderminster, take the bus to Stourport
and walk back but, with a comparative wealth of buses, alternative combin-
ations can be devised.

From the York Street bus-stop in Stourport, turn right and then left along
Bridge Street. Just before the road passes over the River Severn, follow the
slope down left to a car park and (Crown) basin. This wide area of tarmac
eventually leads to the river. Turn left along the river towpath to go past a
funfair. Within a short distance this arrives at the splendid Stourport Basin.

Stourport was effectively created at the behest of James Brindley and the
S & W Canal Company. Before they arrived, the tiny hamlet of Little Mitton

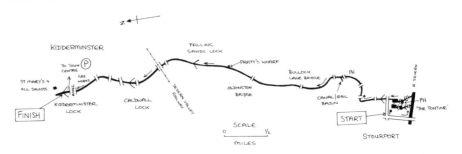

The Staffordshire & Worcestershire Canal

had just a handful of inhabitants. Less than thirty years later (in 1795), the population was more than 1,300 and the town consisted of a series of basins, warehouses, workers' cottages and a developing subsidiary industry. Lower Mitton wasn't Brindley's first choice. He had originally wanted to make his junction with the Severn at Bewdley, an established river port some 4 miles upstream. But partly because of local objections and partly because of the very convenient sandstone levels between Kidderminster and Lower Mitton, modern-day Stourport became what it is.

The two entrances to the canal are now ahead of you. The first can be seen from a humpback bridge over the entrance to a narrow lock. Above it, in a staircase, a second lock lifts the canal boats to the Bottom or Lower Basin. On the left of the second lock is a covered dry lock. Two further staircase narrow locks lift craft to another basin, the Clock Basin. This lies just out of view and to the west of the Clock Warehouse which sits proudly at the centre of the complex. The site of the funfair, by the way, was formerly that of a steam engine which pumped water up into Clock Basin in order to maintain the levels.

Continue along the Severn towpath to reach the 15 ft 4 in wide Barge or Trow Lock. This was the original entrance to the canal from the Severn; the narrow locks were not added until 1781. Ahead of you is the Tontine, a large hotel and inn built in 1788 for the many traders who came here to do business. It was also the place where the S & W management committee periodically met its shareholders. The building is now divided into apartments and yet also still functions as an inn. The gardens afford an excellent spot for a summer's lunch. Ian Langford, in his fine, scholarly towpath guide (see below), explains that a tontine is a type of investment in which the shares become null and void when their owners die. Eventually the sole survivor takes ownership of the property. Whether this father-time version of Russian roulette was used with the Tontine Hotel is unknown.

Cross the barge lock at the top gates to go left of the Tontine to the second barge lock. Ahead is the Upper (sometimes called the Middle) Basin. This is the biggest in the complex and also the oldest, built between 1768 and 1771. On the

Stourport Basin

left is the Clock Warehouse, now home to the Stourport Yacht Club. The clock was apparently a gift from the locals (although the company did chip in) in 1812.

Pass to the right of the Upper Barge Lock and in front of the curved walls of the British Waterways yard (formerly the offices of the Severn & Canal Carrying Company). This shortly leads to a road (Mart Lane). Turn left to a viewing point (formerly the site of a warehouse known as the long room) where on a warm day the seats can be used to good advantage. On the other side of Mart Lane is a timber yard that is on the site of what was formerly the 'Furthermost' Basin. This was used for the unloading of coal destined for Stourport power station (situated on the Severn just a little way downstream). This traffic was finally transferred to the railway in 1949 and the basin filled in.

Our route continues along Mart Lane. The row of terraced workman's cottages on the right was built by the canal company and, although they look rather dilapidated, are listed ancient monuments. The entrance to the S & W is now over to the left. The canal passes York Street by Wallfield Bridge. One of the delights of the S & W is that since the 1830s, all the bridges bear fine oval, cast-iron name and number-plates. They are, without doubt, a useful aid to navigation for both boaters and walkers.

Immediately past the bridge is York Street Lock with its 1853 toll cottage (now converted into a shop). The canal follows a secluded line away from the streets of Stourport, wedged between a high brick wall and the sad remains of the canal company's maintenance yards. We go under Lower Mitton Bridge almost in secrecy, catching just the odd glimpse of the world (and Tesco's) outside. The fine warehouse on the left-hand bank formerly belonged to an iron foundry, the works itself having been demolished in preference for the police and fire stations.

After the busy Gilgal Bridge, the canal seems to be seeking out some more rural resort. The line taken is high above the Stour Valley on a course chosen to be along an easily worked sandstone ledge. As a consequence, the line bends and twists around the contours and there is no more splendid example than the next sudden sharp turn which gives the left-hand bank a cliff-like profile as it rises up to St Michael's churchyard above. An unusually inclined, small pedestrian bridge (Mitton Chapel Bridge, No. 7) crosses the canal on the bend.

The path continues on to pass some canal workers' cottages that date from 1800. After them is the Bird in Hand pub and opposite, after a second look, an allotment full of gravestones, part of St Michael's churchyard. The canal now passes under a wide brick arch bridge that once carried the Severn Valley line. Passenger services between Stourport and Hartlebury were withdrawn on 5 January 1970 although coal traffic continued to use this section until March 1979 *en route* for Stourport power station. On the left just after the bridge is the basin where goods were moved from the railway on to the canal. Steel was imported from South Wales and coal from Highley Colliery near Bewdley and shipped to the Wilden (just across the Stour Valley) and Stourvale (just north of Kidderminster) ironworks. The old pulley wheel, on the towpath side, was used to haul the boats in and out of the basin.

After a while we reach Upper Mitton Bridge (No. 8). Here the canal widens slightly at the site of Upper Mitton Wharf. To the right, through the hedgerow is the River Stour which meanders across the valley almost to run into the towpath; a spill weir provides an overflow from the canal. After Bullock Lane Bridge (No. 9), the canal runs quietly through a pleasantly wooded stretch high above the Stour Valley with the red sandstone occasionally outcropping along the left bank. Oldington Bridge (No. 10) is a fine and typical Brindley accommodation bridge made of brick but with a sandstone block stringer course and coping.

After a short distance, the towpath passes over a small bridge opposite a winding hole or boat-turning point. This is Pratt's Wharf. The bridge is now blocked but it was the entrance to a branch down to the River Stour. In among the trees, shrubs, dead fish and old Coke tins on the right is a derelict lock, built in the 1840s to link the canal to the Stour. At that time, the river was navigable for about a mile downstream to Wilden ironworks. Before the junction was built, the coal and iron were transhipped here into smaller river boats which then completed the journey. The arm was last used in 1949. The Wilden ironworks closed down shortly thereafter and the river is no longer navigable although a towpath can still be followed south to the site of the works which has now become a trading estate.

After a pipe crosses the canal to the sewage works on the left bank (hidden from the eye but not from the nose), the woods thicken and the canal bends around to Falling Sands Lock (No. 4). Before admiring the lock itself, take note of the wrought-iron, cantilever bridge that crosses in front of the lock gates. It has a gap between the two arms to allow the tow line to pass through it, a neat idea which must have saved the bargemen quite a lot of time. Falling Sands Lock is well named as it has been built on an area of unstable wind-blown sands.

After the lock, the canal follows the contours around to reach Falling Sands Bridge which is now, sadly, living up to its name and has been superceded by an ugly, temporary structure. Both are completely upstaged, however, by the magnificent Severn Valley Railway Viaduct which carries the steam railway into Kidderminster. The line was opened on 1 June 1878 to provide a link between the Oxford, Worcester & Wolverhampton Railway (the OW & WR) and the

The Severn Valley Railway Viaduct and Falling Sands Bridge, near Kidderminster on the Staffordshire & Worcestershire Canal

Severn Valley line at Bewdley. On 5 January 1970 it went the same way as the Stourport line. However, this line has been splendidly restored by enthusiasts from the Severn Valley Railway and now runs up to Bridgnorth. The viaduct spanning the Stour can be seen on the right.

The town of Kidderminster is now becoming increasingly obvious: a car scrap-yard occupies the right-hand view while the path consists of a series of concrete slabs each labelled 'Danger 132,000 volts'. Fortunately the scene is saved by the marvellous Caldwell Lock which appears to have been hewn out of solid rock. A split, cantilever, bridge again precedes the lock but there was also, at one time, a house built into the cliff. A small remnant of this looking like a fireplace can be seen just above the downstream lock gate. The house collapsed in the 1960s following years of vandalism and neglect. One can only wonder how the lock was built into the sandstone cliff which rises so strikingly behind it.

The stretch between here and central Kidderminster was the site of an interesting experiment in the 1920s. The company set up an electric barge, drawing power from overhead lines, to pull boats into town at a steady $3\frac{1}{2}$ miles per hour. Although successful at hauling the barges, the idea was never adopted, presumably because of the capital cost involved in putting up the overhead lines.

After a modern road bridge carries the A451 over the canal, the left bank contains the remains of Old Foundry Wharf and the last remnants of a brass and iron foundry that was closed in 1972. How long those remnants will remain is uncertain but a former coal wharf about 100 yd further along on the left has certainly reverted to nature. The canal passes under another bridge (Caldwall Mill Bridge, No. 14) to an old wharf now used as a car park and then to a metal girder bridge which carries Castle Street.

High walls line the canal and towpath. Here, as a path comes down from Castle Street, is the Kidderminster Public Wharf. The buildings to the right are one part of Kidderminster's famous carpet industry (in this case Brinton's). This stretch offers those interested in Victorian factory architecture a wonderful time. As the towpath swings gently left, the view is dominated by the terrific sight of the old gas works and its wonderful chimney. The area was a busy one for the canal as the towpath passes over a series of blocked-off factory arms. The timber yard across the waterway also used the S & W extensively.

We are now close to the centre of Kidderminster. After passing under a modern road bridge that carries the A442 to Bridgnorth, the canal reaches Town (or Kidderminster) Lock, which at 12 ft is one of the deepest on the line. The scene, overlooked by St Mary and All Saints Church, was once a busy one. Here was Mill Wharf, said to have been the centre of the canal's activities in the area, with a series of warehouses, a weighbridge and a stables. There was also a coal wharf for the carpet factory on the left-hand bank. From here the horse-drawn fly-boats left at 6 p.m. in the evening, loaded with Kidderminster carpet for the railway station at Wolverhampton, from where they were shipped out for distribution. It's remarkable that this activity continued until October 1950. Unfortunately, the most remarkable thing now is the traffic noise.

Before returning under the bridge and going left into the town centre, it's worth going a bit further along the canal to see the River Stour passing quietly, and mostly unloved, underneath a small aqueduct. Kidderminster itself is full of shops, cafés, take-aways and pubs. The Town Hall bus-stops are at the opposite end of the pedestrianized shopping centre.

Further Explorations

Virtually all 46 miles of the S & W are open to walkers (the only difficult stretch is that between Aldersley and Hatherton Junctions) and nearly all of it is worth a stroll or a visit.

The area between Kidderminster and Stourton (OS Landranger 139, ref: SO 861848) has some magnificent sandstone scenery and is full of interest. An excellent walk of 11½ miles goes from Kidderminster Lock to Stourbridge with return by train. The route initially passes through wooded stretches around Wolverley and heads on to Cookley. Just before this small town the canal does an almost 180° turn before reaching Debdale Lock with its intriguing cave storehouse and circular weir. After passing an ironworks, the canal goes under the town through what is thought to be the oldest navigable tunnel on the waterway system. Shortly after the tunnel, the canal bends around Austcliff, a sheer rock overhang, and on to the Whittington Locks and Kinver. After passing the Hyde, the canal goes through some delightful country to the diminutive Dunsley Tunnel. From Stewponey Lock, with its octagonal toll-house, the canal reaches the Stourbridge Canal. This line takes the waterway via the Dudley Canal into Birmingham, a through route first opened in 1792. Turn right to cross the bridge to go along the Stourbridge. This passes two locks, changes banks at a road bridge, passes two more locks and then continues to Wordsley Junction (about 2 miles). Here cross a bridge and turn right to follow the Stourbridge branch into town.

The area around Bratch (near Wombourne) is interesting and can provide a gentle stroll up and down the canal of about 2 miles. Park at the well signposted Bratch picnic-site car park (OS Landranger 139, ref: SJ 867938) and walk north (i.e. turn right at the canal). Virtually immediately, you reach Bratch Locks. Here is an attractive octagonal toll-cottage and three locks, each with a large side pound (to the left), built to ensure that there is sufficient water to operate the locks which are very close together. Walk north along the canal to the highly unusual bridge at Aw. The lock here also has one of Brindley's famous circular weirs. A notice back at the picnic site has information on the splendid Victorian waterworks pumping station (built here for easy access to coal from the canal) and the nearby Kingswinford Railway Path (ably described in Jeff Vinter, *Railway Walks: LMS*. Alan Sutton Publishing).

At the northern end, the S & W joins the Trent & Mersey Canal at Great Haywood Junction (OS Landranger 127, ref: SJ 995229). There is a good walk between the junction and Milford Bridge (968241), a distance of $2\frac{1}{4}$ miles each way. There is ample parking at Milford village green and some on street at Great Haywood. At the junction, the S & W is crossed by a proud and elegant roving bridge which carries the T & M's towpath. This is immediately followed by a toll-house with some fine windows and then two aqueducts, the second of which passes over the Trent. After a bridge, the canal widens to form Tixall Wide, a broad made to satisfy the demands of the local landowner, Thomas Clifford of Tixall Hall, who was also one of the original principal investors in the waterway. It's a very pleasant spot and some authors have described it as the most beautiful part of the waterway network. After Tixall Lock and a road bridge, the route crosses the River Sow by a typical Brindley aqueduct, the low arches producing a squat, heavy appearance. The walk ends at Milford Bridge, a turnover bridge where towing horses could change banks without needing to uncouple their tow-lines. Those with OS maps could devise a return across the neighborough-ing Cannock Chase to meet the Trent & Mersey, and then back to Great Haywood.

Further Information

The S & W Canal Society can be found at:
c/o Mrs A. Pollard,
8 Frimstones Street,
Wollaston,
Stourbridge,
West Midlands.

For more information about the canal, the following books can be recommended:
Langford, J. Ian, *Staffordshire & Worcestershire Canal, Towpath Guide No. 1*. Goose & Son Publishers, 1974.
Hadfield, Charles, *The Canals of the West Midlands*. David & Charles, 1969.

10
THE STRATFORD-UPON-AVON CANAL

Kingswood to Stratford

Introduction

Pick any tourist at random from the thronging hordes that pack around the Memorial Theatre in Stratford and ask them where the canal is and they probably couldn't tell you. Okay, so there's a basin with boats in the middle of Bancroft Gardens but a canal? And where do the boats go when they disappear under the bridge at the north-east corner? Don't they know that within just a few yards of the crowded streets lies a peaceful watery retreat? No, they don't – and long may it be so.

The Stratford-upon-Avon Canal is $25\frac{1}{2}$ miles of narrow canal from a junction with the Worcester & Birmingham at King's Norton to the River Avon at Stratford. The line is broadly divided into two halves geographically, historically and, for many years, legally. Built first, the northern end runs from the Worcester & Birmingham by a guillotine stop lock (designed to prevent excessive loss of water into the W & B) and through Brandwood Tunnel to Warstock and Shirley. From there it leaves suburbia to Earlswood where feeders from the canal's reservoirs top up the level. The last part of the $12\frac{1}{2}$ mile long northern canal runs past Hockley Heath and down the Lapworth Locks to Kingswood Junction where a short arm joins the Grand Union Canal (the former Warwick & Birmingham Canal).

The southern canal is 13 miles long and was built some ten years or so after the northern. By the early 1950s, it was largely derelict and was scheduled for abandonment. Responsibility for it was then taken over by the National Trust who ran it from 1960 until 1988, during which time it was gradually restored to life and water. The first part of the southern canal continues down the Lapworth Locks before running under the M40 and into some peaceful, rural countryside. There now follow three fine iron-trough aqueducts: Yarningale, Wootton

Wawen and Edstone (Bearley). After further lockage at Wilmcote, the line runs gently and secretively into Stratford to meet the Avon at Bancroft.

The southern Stratford will always hold a special place in the heart of canal enthusiasts as it was the first to be restored from dereliction in the early 1960s. But even for those who don't have the romantic associations, a walk along the Stratford makes a fine, if fairly long, day out and savours the charm of this fine waterway.

History

The town of Stratford in Warwickshire has always had its own waterway, the River Avon, which flows 42 miles into the River Severn at Tewkesbury. This waterway had been made navigable in 1639 and had become an important route for cargo coming to the Midlands from Bristol. Stratford was also on a major land route for grain passing north and for coal going south. You can imagine, therefore, the shock to the good peoples of the town when, in the late eighteenth century, the opening of the canal systems which joined Birmingham and Bristol, and Coventry and Oxford, caused the traffic that used the Stratford route to drop by 75 per cent. The townsfolk feared they were being bypassed and sought to be returned to life in the mainstream.

In the early 1790s, several different proposals to link Stratford with the burgeoning canal network were the talk of the town. One would have taken a line to the Coventry Canal at Warwick, a second to the Stourbridge Canal. In the event, the committee formed to consider the issue had a straight choice between making a cut to the Digbeth branch of the Birmingham Canal or a line to the, then still to be built, Worcester & Birmingham Canal at King's Norton. The issue finally resolved itself when the proprietors of the Dudley Canal decided to link with the W & B at Selly Oak. This new line, the Dudley No. 2 Canal, promised a cheap source of, and ready traffic in, coal heading from Netherton to the south.

John Snape of Birmingham surveyed a line from the proposed W & B at King's Norton to Stratford that ran close to the new Warwick & Birmingham Canal (now the Grand Union) at Lapworth. This survey included two quarry branches: one from Hockley to Tanworth and the other from Wilmcote to Temple Grafton. In these original plans there was to be no junction with the Avon. Instead, the proposals took the line to a terminus near the present site of Stratford railway station. Charles Hadfield explains that this, apparently strange, decision was taken to offset any possible antagonism from the Worcester & Birmingham who would have feared competition from an alternative River Severn to Birmingham route.

The Stratford-upon-Avon Canal Act was passed on 28 March 1793. It authorized capital of £120,000 with power to raise a further £60,000 if needed. In 1795, a further Act gave powers to raise another £10,000 to build the link between the Stratford and the Warwick & Birmingham at Lapworth. Construction work, under the engineer Josiah Clowes, began in November 1793 from the northern end and proceeded, at least initially, with some vigour. Although Clowes died in 1794, by 25 May 1796 the line was open from King's Norton to Hockley Heath – a distance of $9\frac{3}{4}$ miles. This stretch had no locks but did have the 350 yd long Brandwood Tunnel. Despite the comparative simplicity of the route, the works used the entire authorized capital.

With no finance available, building work slowed to a stop. It wasn't until 1799 that further progress was possible following the passage of another Act which authorized an extra £50,000. This same Act altered the course of the unbuilt section of canal near Lapworth to take it closer to the Warwick & Birmingham. With Samual Potter, formerly Clowes' assistant, appointed as engineer and Benjamin Outram called in to help, building was restarted. By 24 May 1802, the line reached Kingswood (near Lapworth) and the Warwick & Birmingham Canal. The cost to date had totalled £153,000 but, at last, there was a route from the W & B and Dudley Canals in Birmingham through to the south. There was also some prospect of toll income to bolster flagging fortune and enthusiasm.

Meanwhile in 1798, George Perrott, owner of the Lower Avon, made moves to join the canal with the Avon at Bancroft, Stratford. Such plans must have appeared somewhat fanciful at the time with no apparent possibility of raising the funds to get the line anywhere near the town let alone to the Avon. Attempts to raise the extra cash needed to do so failed miserably and it wasn't until 1810 that any further significant progress was possible. The stimulus was the would-be visionary plan to link the Wiltshire & Berkshire Canal with the Stratford to form a new west of central north–south canal line. The line was planned to run via Shipston on Stour, Bourton-on-the-Hill, Lower Swell, Bourton-on-the-Water, Great Rissington, Bampton and Fyfield. Although definitely lodged in the realms of speculation, the scheme took the fancy of one William James, a local land agent and businessman. James, who was already a shareholder in the Stratford Canal, saw the potential for making Stratford into the hub of a nationwide transport system. Whether this was a false vision or not, James' zeal was responsible for a burst of renewed enthusiasm over the ailing Stratford line. In 1810, money was again being raised successfully and, by 1812, construction work was under way once more. On 22 June 1813, the line was open to Wootton Wawen and supplying coal to Alcester.

In September 1813, the route south was adjusted and the plan to join the Avon officially lodged. By now William James was the owner of the Upper Avon Navigation and it was almost certainly with his encouragement that the link was forged in order to compete with the Worcester & Birmingham. This scheme was approved by Act of Parliament in May 1815. The plan, however, had already stimulated competition between the two companies. Initially this was seen simply as a race as to which line could open first, a contest won by the W & B which opened on 4 December 1815. The Stratford wasn't finally complete until the following year and opened on 24 June 1816 with full ceremony. Ironically, on the big day the canal committee had to borrow a boat from the rival W & B to take it from Wootton Wawen to Stratford, where the assembled population duly rejoiced.

The line as opened was $25\frac{1}{2}$ miles long: the northern section from King's Norton to Kingswood was $12\frac{1}{2}$ miles and the southern section into Stratford was 13 miles. The canal is level from its junction with the W & B to Lapworth, it then falls through fifty-four locks to the Avon. As the line from Kingswood to Stratford had cost £143,000, the total cost of the canal was about £297,000.

Although in heavy competition with its neighbours, the Stratford was successful in becoming the main route for the Netherton coal trade and for other goods from the Dudley No. 2 Canal. Iron, firebricks and other industrial products came mainly from the Stourbridge area and even as far away as Coalbrookdale. Salt from Droitwich arrived via the W & B to pass along the Stratford to Lapworth. The bulk of the trade to Stratford and the surrounding areas, however, was coal and return cargo was primarily agricultural produce (such as malt and corn). Although the branches to the quarries were never built, land transport brought limestone, paving stones and 'marble' to the canal. The Temple Grafton limestone was mostly shipped to Halesowen, where it was used in the ironworks, and to limekilns at Selly Oak and Haywood. There were also limeworks at Stratford.

The expected competition with the W & B for trade between Birmingham and the Severn was soon lost. The Stratford was simply too indirect and the Avon far too circuitous to attract any through custom and none was found. The whole issue was sealed in 1830 when the W & B Company leased the lower Avon, effectively closing off the through route for good, although competition remained for the carriage of coal to the Evesham area. Despite this, the Avon link was important to the canal. Throughout the 1830s, some 10,000 tons of coal p.a. were transhipped from the cut to the river at Bancroft. The canal also benefitted from the Stratford & Moreton horse tramway which carried coal (16–19,000 tons p.a. in the 1830s) on to Moreton-in-Marsh (14 miles to the south) and, later, to Shipston on Stour.

By 1838 the canal was carrying over 180,000 tons of goods p.a. and averaging annual gross receipts of £13,500. Dividends had been paid since 1824 and, in the 1830s, fluctuated between 30s. and £2 per share. But the 1830s were the peak years for the Stratford Canal and profitability was soon to decline in the face of railway competition. There had also been some significant positioning and counter positioning by the various canal companies, most notably the W & B and the Warwick & Birmingham, in order to compete for traffic and to promote or dissuade the various new schemes that were appearing – the most

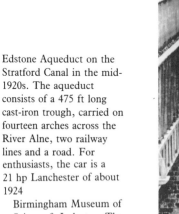

Edstone Aqueduct on the Stratford Canal in the mid-1920s. The aqueduct consists of a 475 ft long cast-iron trough, carried on fourteen arches across the River Alne, two railway lines and a road. For enthusiasts, the car is a 21 hp Lanchester of about 1924
Birmingham Museum of Science & Industry, The Boat Museum archive

notable of which was a new London to Birmingham line. But it was the direct competition with the railways which bit deepest into the company's profits. To compete with the London & Birmingham Railway, which opened in 1838, both the Stratford and the Warwick & Birmingham cut their tolls and thereby reduced their profitability. Despite this, Stratford in 1845 was a trading centre of note. There were twenty-two merchants operating from the town in coal, corn and timber: 50,000 tons of coal were still being shipped into the town, 15,000 tons travelling on via the tramway and 8,000 on via the Avon, 16,000 tons of limestone were still being shipped out from Wilmcote.

The company took an honest stance in the face of the increasingly overpowering railway competition. On 22 March 1845, it agreed to be taken over by the Oxford, Worcester & Wolverhampton Railway which planned to build a line from Birmingham, through Stratford and Moreton to Cheltenham. However, as part of this arrangement it was agreed that if the OW & WR could not get its Act to authorize the purchase then the Great Western Railway would be allowed to step into the breach to do a deal on its own behalf or as an agent.

In 1846, the OW & WR and the Birmingham and Oxford Junction Railway agreed that the latter would build a railway to the north of the Stratford whereas the former would build a line to the south. As a result, the OW & WR's Act of July 1846 included powers for the OW & WR to buy the canal for the B & OJ. The Act laid down clauses to ensure that the canal was maintained and that tolls should not be higher than they were at the time of the Act. Typically tolls for coal and goods taken between King's Norton and Stratford were 1½d. per ton per mile with goods taken as back carriage tolled at ¾d. The OW & WR, however, found that due to a problem with the Birmingham & Oxford Junction Bill passed in the same session, it was unable to sell the canal immediately to the B & OJ and hence delayed its purchase until the B & OJ had legal powers to own and run a canal. Unfortunately, repeated bills were thrown out of Parliament and the situation ran on unsatisfactorily.

In 1848, the B & OJ was bought by the Great Western Railway, changed its mind about the usefulness of owning the canal and became obstructive to the OW & WR, which suddenly found that it was committed to buying a canal it didn't want. The purchase was finally cemented on 1 January 1856 although the line was not worked by the OW & WR until 1 May 1857. In 1859, the OW & WR raised £160,000 to pay off the canal's annuities, mortgages and other debts still outstanding.

There was no doubt that the purchase was a mistake for the OW & WR. The canal was soon to begin its inevitable decline. Most of the traffic gradually seeped away on to the nearby railway line and little or no dredging was done to maintain the course. While not actively discouraging traffic, there were no positive efforts to attract through cargo, primarily as this would have competed with the railway traffic. The Stratford-upon-Avon Railway was opened on 10 October 1860 with stations at Bearley and Wilmcote and on to Birmingham. By 1861, the OW & WR had been renamed the West Midland Railway and railway traffic could pass straight through Stratford from Evesham. Canal receipts dropped by 20 per cent.

On 1 August 1863, the old antagonist, the GWR took over the West Midland and hence control of the Stratford Canal. As was inevitable with the GWR, canal traffic declined dramatically. Receipts fell from an average of £6,760 p.a. in the early 1860s to under £2,000 in the late 1880s. By the 1890s, traffic on the southern section was all but gone while that on the northern part was very much reduced. Traffic in the 1890s was mostly in manure with a small amount of coal, lime, grain and salt. When Temple Thurston passed this way in 1911, the locks were seldom used and rapidly weeding up.

Somehow the line survived until nationalization in 1948 although the southern half had been unnavigable since the Second World War. The last boat to reach Stratford did so in the early 1930s. In the Board of Survey report of 1955, it was recommended that the northern section be retained while the southern was put into the 'insufficient justification to keep' category. This official classification must have stimulated the Warwickshire County Council to consider the canal dead and, in 1958, to announce its closure so that repairs could be undertaken on Wilmcote Bridge. This act was the spur needed for the recovery of the waterway. Meetings of the recently formed Stratford-upon-Avon Canal Society were held to protest against the abandonment of the waterway and a use permit, issued for a canoe trip from Stratford to Earlswood, proved that the line was still a navigable canal.

Stopping the abandonment was one thing, restoring it was another. The canal society, in league with the Inland Waterways Association, proposed that the National Trust should take over the canal with the purpose of undertaking the restoration. The trust, who expressed interest in a number of canals at that time, agreed to take on the responsibility and, after the official withdrawal of the closure plan in 1959, took a lease on the southern section of the Stratford on 29 September 1960. With funds from the British Transport Commission, the Ministry of Transport, gifts from other supporters as well as from the National Trust itself, a programme of restoration was implemented under the control of David Hutchings. The sterling work of the volunteer effort (which included prisoners from Winson Green prison) was rewarded when the Queen Mother reopened the line on 11 July 1964. The line is a model restoration for all that have followed since.

The Queen Mother reopens the restored southern Stratford-upon-Avon Canal amid great celebration on 11 July 1964

Birmingham Post & Mail, British Waterways

Once fully restored, the role of the National Trust was always slightly anachronistic, particularly as its control was limited to the southern half. Responsibility was therefore transferred to British Waterways in May 1988. Since then the line has formed part of the highly popular Avon Ring circuit that allows boaters to motor from Stratford along the River Avon to Tewkesbury, then along the River Severn to Worcester, then up the Worcester & Birmingham to King's Norton and then back to the beginning along the Stratford.

The Walk

Start: Lapworth railway station (OS ref: SP 188716)
Finish: Bancroft Gardens, Stratford (OS ref: SP 204548)
Distance: 14½ miles/23 km (or shorter, see text)
Maps: OS Landranger 151 (Stratford-upon-Avon) and 139 (Birmingham)
Return: BR Stratford to Lapworth via Hatton. Some go direct, otherwise change at Hatton. Stay on same platform for train to Lapworth which goes in opposite direction. Telephone: (021) 2002601

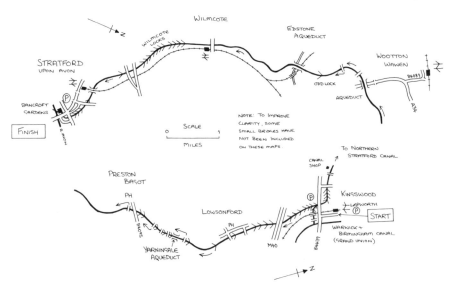

The Stratford-upon-Avon Canal

Car parks: Various and well-signposted at Stratford, including Stratford station or Lapworth station
Public transport: Lapworth is on the main Oxford to Birmingham New Street BR line

This long walk can be made shorter in a number of ways using stations at Wootton Wawen (a $\frac{1}{2}$ mile from the canal) and Wilmcote. The route can be divided into two ($7\frac{1}{2}$ and 8 miles) using Wootton Wawen. As the most interesting canal structure along the route is between Wootton Wawen and Wilmcote, a 4 mile walk between the two stations will include this sight.

Lapworth to Wootton Wawen

From Lapworth station cross the line and turn right to pass along this residential road to a T-junction. Turn left for about a 100 yd to reach a bridge. Just before The Navigation pub, cross the road to turn right along the towpath which is on the right-hand bank.

This is the Grand Union Canal (formerly the Warwick & Birmingham) which, to the south, continues on to London and, to the north, goes to Birmingham where it splits at Bordesley Junction. One line continues to Digbeth. The other passes along the Birmingham & Warwick Junction Canal to join the Birmingham & Fazeley Canal at Salford Junction almost directly under the spaghetti junction of the M6.

If you're getting confused with all these junctions, life will shortly get worse because the walk soon reaches Kingswood Junction which comes in from the right. The main line of the Warwick & Birmingham now runs straight on south via the Hatton Locks to Warwick (see Further Explorations). Here we cross the junction roving bridge and turn right.

This short length of junction canal was opened on 24 May 1802 and, for ten years, was the southern exit of the Stratford. After passing under the railway, the canal bends right just before a lock. Originally the line ran straight on here through a lock, which was to the right of the building on the other side of the fence, to a basin. The lock had a fall of 6 ft thereby ensuring that the Warwick & Birmingham gained water at every downstream passage. When the Stratford company restarted construction work in 1812, they built a lock (now called lock 21) on the main line above the old basin, lowered the level of the basin itself to that of the branch (and hence of the W & B) and removed the top gates of the old lock. These were replaced by a stop lock with guillotine gates and a channel through which water could flow from the Stratford to the W & B. This revision angered the W & B who probably felt that they would gain less water and may even lose some if the level of the W & B were higher. The row rumbled on for several years before it was decided to build the present lock which runs to the level above No. 21. The original channel was then closed, filled in and converted into a private garden. The new line and lock were opened on 22 December 1818 and effectively restored the *status quo*.

After passing the lock, the vista opens out to the small lagoon which is Lapworth lower reservoir. The route to Stratford (13 miles) can be gained by turning left. However, it's well worth taking a short stroll up to see the Lapworth Locks and the northern Stratford. So cross the southern canal entrance roving bridge in front of you and bear right to pass a car park and picnic site on the left (toilets can be found here). The towpath passes a lock and the upper Lapworth reservoir to go under a road bridge that carries the B4439. The canal now bends around to the left to pass four locks. As the locks in the flight are very close together, each is provided with a sizeable side pound to ensure that sufficient water is available for continuous operation. Following a pipe bridge, there is a superb view up the Lapworth flight (Locks 8–14). After a photo-call and a visit to the small canal shop on the left, return to the entrance of the southern canal.

From the roving bridge, the canal runs down to pass lock 21. Immediately, the right bank of the canal widens to a reed-filled mire. This is the site of the original Harborough Banks Basin. The original route of the junction to the W & B can be seen on the towpath side of the canal where there is now a brick wall.

One of the most interesting characteristic features of the southern Stratford Canal can be seen from this point. On the towpath side of the canal just beyond the brick wall is a typical southern Stratford lock house – a unique design with its curved or barrel-vaulted roof built like the brick arch of a bridge. The barrel is held together with steel cross-ties that link the walls. It's said that these delightful little cottages were built by navvies who knew how to make tunnels and bridges but weren't too hot on the normal methods of building a house. Whatever the story, there are a number of them along the southern canal. Many have been extended in various ways although some remain, as the builders intended, a delightful and unique piece of architecture.

The towpath passes six locks altogether before becoming embroiled in the ugliest bridge on the line, on the new M40. The noise from the motorway engulfs what must have been a very remote part of the canal at one time. It's still very lovely now but we have to walk another $\frac{1}{4}$ mile before the rumble subsides and the birds become the loudest thing around. The second lock after the motorway is number 28. Here the residents of the barrel-roofed lock-cottage have set up a small canalware shop. These traditional designs are not to everybody's taste but there is a fine collection on display and for sale.

We pass the abutments of an ex-GWR railway bridge (which joined Lapworth with Henley-in-Arden), a lock, a bridge and another lock before entering

Lowsonford. Here, conveniently is the Fleur de Lys pub on the opposite bank. This can be reached by crossing at the next road bridge.

At the next lock (No. 31), there is another barrel-roofed cottage still owned by the National Trust. At the next lock, the towpath changes sides. Shortly thereafter is Yarningale Aqueduct, the first of three iron aqueducts between here and Stratford. This is the second aqueduct to be built on the site. The original structure was washed away on 28 July 1934 when the Grand Union burst its banks and caused the small stream that runs underneath the Stratford to flood. The new structure was made, in what must have been record time, by the Horseley ironworks in Birmingham and the canal was reopened on 23 August. It consists of a series of cast-iron sections which have been bolted together to form a kind of trough through which the waterway flows across the stream. In the restoration of the southern canal in the early 1960s, the brick abutments were restored by inmates from Winson Green prison. The sunken towpath along the side of the aqueduct gives walkers an unusual view as the

Yarningale Aqueduct

waterway comes up to eye level (depending on your height of course) before returning to normal on the other side.

Four locks further on (at lock 37), the canal runs past arguably the most extraordinary extension to a barrel-roofed cottage on the line. This one has been privately owned since before the National Trust took control of the waterway. Here also are the Haven Tea Rooms.

Just before lock 38 take the path through the hedge to the left and turn right along the road and then back down to the canal at the bridge. This is Preston Bagot. If thirsty turn right across the bridge to the Crab Mill pub. The towpath, meanwhile, passes under a road bridge to cross the canal at the footbridge a little further on. The line now enters some remote countryside and wanders around the contours for about 2 miles before reaching Wootton Wawen.

Wootton Wawen to Stratford

For those joining from Wootton Wawen station, make your way to the A34 main road and turn right. Walk on for about a ½ mile to a point where the road dips to go under an iron bridge which is in fact an aqueduct carrying the Stratford Canal. There is a small track which runs up the right-hand side of the aqueduct to the canal. Turn right for Stratford.

For those who have walked from Lapworth, Wootton Wawen is first announced by the large Anglo-Welsh boatyard with its tall office building which dominates the left-hand bank. The canal reached Wootton Wawen on 22 June 1813 and the village soon became an important inland port. The boatyard is situated on the site of the wharf built to tranship cargo before the line was fully opened. From September 1814 until June 1816, a horse-drawn tramway was employed to carry coal from here into Stratford. Just after the boatyard, the canal narrows to cross the busy A34 via another iron-trough aqueduct. Carried on two brick-built piers this structure has been here since October 1813. This longevity has been achieved despite the attention of various lorries that have ploughed into it over the years. One such accident in 1968 took two cast-iron girders out of the structure leading to closure of the road. Remarkably they were replaced by modern steel versions within two days thanks to the efforts of a variety of volunteers. Since then the bridge has been hit twice more, although with less significant effect. In all cases, the canal trough remained intact. One good thing about the M40 is that it has removed a large amount of the traffic so that such incidents may be less likely to happen in the future.

Although Wootton Wawen Aqueduct has charm, the best is yet to come. After bending left, the canal heads off south through a slight cutting (after which the towpath changes sides) to the isolated lock known as 'Odd Lock' (No.

Wootton Wawen Aqueduct and the Anglo Welsh boatyard on the Stratford-upon-Avon Canal

39). Shortly thereafter is Edstone or Bearley Aqueduct. Built in 1815, this is another iron-trough structure but on a much grander scale compared with the two already crossed. The Stratford-upon-Avon Canal Society inform me that Edstone Aqueduct is 475 ft or 145 m long (other sources, interestingly, quote anything from 521 ft to 754 ft). It was designed by William Whitmore who was the engineer responsible for the southern half of the canal. It's a splendid sight as its fourteen arches span over the River Alne, the two lines of the Stratford to Birmingham railway and the minor Bearley to Little Alne road. At one time another railway, a branch to Alcester, also ran underneath. Notes from the canal society say that the engine that worked the line was housed under the aqueduct and used water from the canal. As on the other two aqueducts, the towpath is lower than the canal to give walkers an interesting view of boats passing alongside.

After passing a cottage (the site of the former Bearley Wharf), the canal twists round the contours towards Wilmcote. Just before Wilmcote Bridge was the former stone wharf. Limestone was carried 4 miles from the quarries at Temple Grafton to the canal by means of a horse tramway. In 1845, some 16,000 tons of limestone were shipped in this way. The original plan had been for a canal branch but presumably the tramway was less of a financial risk for what was possibly a transient business.

The bridge at Wilmcote is Featherbed Lane Bridge or, more prosaically, No. 59. The poor condition of a former occupant of this site was given as the reason for the warrant for abandonment of the canal presented by Warwickshire County Council in 1958. From this came the restoration movement and the gradual reopening of the southern line. Such restoration includes this section of the towpath which was completely rebuilt by volunteers in the early 1980s. The bridge itself was rebuilt somewhat earlier but also looks to be in fine fettle. Those who wish to utilize Wilmcote station should go up to the road and turn left (turn right for Mary Arden's house).

Over the next 3 miles, the canal passes down the eleven locks that constitute the Wilmcote flight. Thereafter the canal enters Stratford by the back door, squeezed between various industrial estates and even Stratford Town football ground. After two bridges carry the train lines into Stratford railway station, the canal secretly eases its way into the centre of town.

The stretch around the next lock (No. 52) was formerly the site of Kendalls, a supplier of chemicals to the brewing industry. Their first works were on the towpath side of lock 52. However, a new factory was built on the opposite bank just after the next two bridges and before lock 53. This spot is now occupied by private dwellings. Both sites received supplies of chemicals via the canal, and Nick Billingham has reported, in *Waterways World*, that the trade continued at least up to the First World War.

The canal now descends rapidly via three locks to reach a bridge carrying the busy A46. Go under this and immediately over a small turnover bridge to the opposite bank where there are some new retirement flats. Follow the path to reach another bridge. Here the towpath ends, so go up some steps and cross the two lanes of the road to reach Bancroft Gardens. The canal basin here can be followed around to the final lock (No. 56) and a small bridge that was rebuilt by prisoners during the great restoration. Just beyond is the River Avon.

Bancroft was originally the site of two basins and a major port. The second basin was on the spot now occupied by the theatre and was filled in when the original building was put up in the 1870s (the present theatre dates from the early 1930s). The waterway link between the two basins ran straight on from the point where the canal enters the modern basin from under the bridge (i.e. parallel with Waterside). Cargo was unloaded here both for Stratford and for transhipment south via the Stratford & Moreton Horse Railway. A wagon that once ran on the line is permanently sited by the path on the side furthest away from the theatre. The tramway itself ran along this path and across the bridge, now used as a pedestrian route to the sports grounds and car parks on the other side of the Avon. The canal company buildings that lined the basin have been cleared and the area is more often than not awash with tourists and theatre-goers all wondering where the boats go after they turn right out of the basin.

Further Explorations

Sadly, the only portion of the northern Stratford that is walkable throughout is the 2½ miles from Lapworth to Hockley Heath. It is not possible therefore to explore much of the length between Lapworth and King's Norton. Luckily the proximity of the Warwick & Birmingham Canal means that if you are in the area, there's plenty of good towpathing to be had.

The Warwick & Birmingham Canal Act received its Royal Assent on 6 March 1793. It authorized a line from Saltisford in Warwick to the Digbeth Branch of the Birmingham Canal, a distance of just over 22 miles. The canal was fully opened on 19 March 1800, the same day as the Warwick & Napton Canal which took the line on from Saltisford to the Napton Junction to Birmingham. On Canal. This then became the shortest route from London to Birmingham. On 1 January 1929, the W & B merged with the W & N and the Grand Junction and others to form the Grand Union Canal Company.

The recommended walk is of 4 miles from Warwick to Hatton railway station. There is free car parking at both stations and very regular trains between the two. Starting at Warwick, return from the car park to the main road. Turn left and continue for about a ⅓ mile until the road goes over the canal. On the far side of the bridge, take the towpath left. From here the line passes through the outskirts of Warwick to the Saltisford arm and then bends around right to the start of the splendid Hatton Locks. There are twenty-one locks in the Hatton flight, traditionally known as the 'stairway to heaven', between Saltisford and Hatton station. One of the interesting things about them is that they were originally narrow locks. In 1934, they were widened as part of a scheme to attract Birmingham to London traffic back on to the canals. The narrow locks are clearly visible in the massive lock structures although they have all either been filled in or converted into weirs.

There is a brief respite at the top of the main flight when the canal reaches the British Waterways' yard. Those in need of refreshment after the up-hill stretch should go over the stile to the left of the BW yard and through the field into the garden of The Waterman. For those not so tempted, the towpath changes sides at the bridge next to the yard and then goes past the final four locks in the flight.

The line then passes through gentle countryside for about 1 mile before Hatton railway station can be seen on the left. Go up on the far side of the bridge and the entrance to the station is in front of you.

Further Information

The Stratford-upon-Avon Canal Society was formed in 1956 with the main aim of ensuring that the southern section of the canal was saved. This objective culminated in the reopening of the line in 1964. Even though its objective has long since been achieved, the society still thrives, meets regularly and publishes a newsletter. Among the activities has been the restoration of certain sections of the towpath. Walkers should therefore be pleased to support them. Their address is:

Stratford-upon-Avon Canal Society,
'Santa Monica',
Earlswood,
Solihull,
West Midlands,
B94 6AQ.

The society publishes its own forty-page guide to the canal which contains a lot of interesting snippets about the line, its history and its restoration.

For detailed history buffs, the Stratford, the Avon and the Stratford & Moreton Railway are described in:
Hadfield, C. and Norris, J., *Waterways to Stratford*. David & Charles, 1968.

The history of the Warwick & Birmingham Canals is ably described in:
Faulkner, A., *The Warwick Canals*. The Railway and Canal Historical Society, 1985.

11
THE TRENT & MERSEY CANAL
Stoke-on-Trent to Kidsgrove

Introduction

A stroll through the centre of some grubby eighteenth-century potteries, a steelworks and a range of old and derelict buildings doesn't sound very promising but, in this walk, we head directly for the heart of the Trent & Mersey Canal. Here is the industry for which the canal was built and the industry which grew on what the canal could feed it. Although large areas have been landscaped, evidence of just how busy the line must have been in its heyday abounds. The whole stretch between Stoke and Longport is littered with old wharves and redundant canal arms. Here are the earthly remains of a busy and profitable waterway, the very origins of the nation's canal network.

At its eastern end, the Trent & Mersey Canal leaves the River Trent at Derwent Mouth where the Derwent joins the Trent just a few miles south of Long Eaton. Within 1 mile, it reaches the canal port of Shardlow, a village effectively created by the T & M, and then continues west along the Trent Valley, past the former entrance to the Derby Canal, and on to Burton-on-Trent. At this point the T & M becomes a narrow canal built to Brindley's 7 ft 'gauge'. Heading south-west, the route passes through Alrewas to reach the first of the important junctions with routes to the south. At Fradley, the junction is with the Coventry Canal – the way, via the northern Oxford and the Grand Union, to London. The T & M now leaves the Trent Valley to turn west and then north-west. After going through Rugeley, the line reaches Great Haywood, the junction with the Staffordshire & Worcestershire Canal and the way, via the River Severn, to Bristol.

After Stone, the canal meets its *raison d'être* at Stoke. In the midst of the Potteries at Etruria, the site of Wedgwood's factory, the Caldon Canal leaves the T & M to run north-east to Leek and Froghall. Meanwhile, boats on the main line continue, past the many redundant pottery works and through Telford's historic Harecastle Tunnel, to reach Kidsgrove. Here the Macclesfield Canal leaves at Hardings Wood Junction only then to go over the T & M at Red Bull Aqueduct. The main line, however, continues through the Cheshire salt fields where, in many places, mining subsidence has severely affected the course of the canal. At Middlewich, a branch goes off to join with the Shropshire Union Canal. After passing through Northwich the line comes close to the Weaver Navigation at Anderton where, to link the two waterways, a massive boat lift was built. The canal then runs through three tunnels to join the Bridgewater Canal. One arm now goes on to Manchester and the other to Runcorn, where nowadays it sadly comes to a dead end, a metaphorical stone's throw away from the Mersey.

Finally, before you venture forth, you should perhaps be aware that, according to Jean Lindsay, the Trent & Mersey Canal Company's motto, as inscribed on its seal, has the natural and idiomatic translation of 'May it flood the countryside and drown the population'. Don't say I didn't warn you.

History

It was the Bridgewater Canal which inspired Josiah Wedgwood, potter and entrepreneur extraordinaire, to see the value of building an artificial waterway to

The pottery industry thrived along the Trent & Mersey corridor in and around Stoke. It used the canal both for the import of china and clay and flint, and for the gentle export of its goods to the world. This picture from Longport in the early 1900s shows the huge numbers of bottle kilns that spread around the canal

British Waterways

connect his new factory at Burslem with the outside world. The Bridgewater, built to service the coal mines around Worsley, was the first man-made canal to be both of utilitarian value and highly profitable. The shrewd Wedgwood foresaw the immense benefit of having a line of his own to bring in china clay from the West Country and to export his delicate products to the rest of Britain and the world.

A canal to link the Rivers Mersey and Weaver with the Trent had first been raised in 1755 (before the Bridgewater) by two northern businessmen who sponsored a survey. Little is known of their plan or why it foundered but the idea was revived in 1758 when James Brindley was asked to survey a line from Stoke-on-Trent to Wilden ferry (on the Trent near Nottingham) by Thomas Broade, Lord Anson and Earl Gower. Brindley's survey, of what he called the Grand Trunk, suggested the possibility of linking the 'Cheshire rivers with the River Severn and finally to connect the Counties through which the R. Trent flows with all parts of the Kingdom'. The first map of the proposed Grand Trunk, which was drawn by Hugh Henshall and approved by John Smeaton, was produced in 1760. It described a route from Longbridge, near Burslem, to Wilden ferry. Smeaton later produced his own survey in which two important features were added: a proposal to extend the line to the River Weaver and a plan to tunnel through the summit at Harecastle.

Whether any of these plans would have come to fruition without the skills and enthusiasm of Josiah Wedgwood is open to question, for nothing appears to have happened until the idea came to his attention in 1765. Wedgwood had discussed the potential for a canal network with two influential friends, Erasmus Darwin (in London) and Thomas Bentley (in the north-west), and had been in contact with Earl Gower concerning Brindley's survey. He now became the guiding light in the venture and it was his abilities and, perhaps a new skill in those times, public relations efforts that drove the project forward. In April 1765, a plan was issued and touted by those interested in the scheme. The canal was to be 76 miles long from Wilden to the River Weaver at Frodsham. It was to be built on the Bridgewater model for boats 6 ft wide and 70 ft long.

There now followed a period during which the precise line taken in Cheshire was under much debate. The original proposal to enter the Weaver was challenged by a new idea that the canal should join with an extension of the Bridgewater Canal, a link which would facilitate a convenient line to Manchester and possibly to Liverpool. It was this latter feature which swung the matter. At a meeting at Wolseley Bridge on 30 December 1765, under the patronage of Earl Gower, a line through to the Mersey (at or near the Runcorn gap) was described, with the cost estimated as being £101,000. Although branches, including one to the River Severn, were discussed, it was concluded that they were not to be part of the matter in hand and were excluded from any proposals.

On 15 January 1766, a petition for the Trent & Mersey Canal was presented to the Commons and the Act received royal assent on 14 May. The company was given permission to raise £130,000 by 650 shares of £200 each. The Act also allowed an extra £20,000 to be raised if needed. On 26 July, Josiah Wedgwood ceremonially cut the first sod at Burslem and the work began both at the Derwent Mouth Junction with the navigable Trent (near Long Eaton) and at the Harecastle Tunnel.

By 1767, concerns were already being expressed about the health of James Brindley, whom Wedgwood, for one, thought was over-doing things. Despite this, Brindley was confident enough about the works to bet his committee that the entire canal would be open by Christmas 1772. Things were certainly progressing well for, by June 1770, the canal was open from Derwent Mouth to the Great Haywood Junction with the Staffordshire & Worcestershire Canal. On 12 November 1771, it was open to Stone (about 8 miles south of Stoke). Charles Hadfield reports that celebrations at the opening of the canal at Stone were rather over-exuberant. The repeated firing of a cannon caused a newly built bridge and lock to collapse. The canal had been open for traffic as early as September 1770 with vessels setting out from Great Haywood every Monday and Thursday morning for Weston-upon-Trent (about 5 miles up from Derwent Mouth). The T & M was thus a going concern and successfully raised a further £70,000 following the passage of a new Act.

On 27 September 1772, James Brindley, the father of the modern canal system, died and Hugh Henshall, Brindley's brother-in-law who had been involved with the T & M from the outset, took over as engineer. By now the canal ran from the Trent right through to the Potteries, a distance of 48 miles. But Brindley's bet would have been lost. The canal from Harecastle to Sandbach wasn't open until April 1775 and Henshall was experiencing severe geological problems at the Cheshire end between Middlewich and Acton. This matter was resolved by building two extra tunnels and the whole line was opened in May 1777. The final cost was £296,600. The finished canal was just over 93 miles long with a rise of 326 ft by thirty-five locks (later increased to thirty-six) from Preston Brook to Harecastle and a fall of 316 ft to Derwent Mouth. Most of the canal was built to Brindley's original 7 ft width but the stretches from Wilden ferry to Burton and from Middlewich to Preston Bridge were 14 ft wide in order to carry river barges of 40 tons burden.

The effect of the canal on the Potteries was both immediate and substantial. Prosperity came to what was once a relatively backward and remote area. Enormous quantities of china clay (from Devon and Cornwall) and flint (from Gravesend and Newhaven) were brought in via the Mersey for the pottery industry. Even the local farms benefitted from the now readily available supply of horse manure that was shipped out from the cities. In 1836, it was recorded that the outward traffic was 61,000 tons to Liverpool (of which 51,000 were earthenware and china), 59,500 tons to Manchester (of which 30,000 were bricks and tiles and 25,000 coal) and 42,000 tons to London (30,000 tons coal and 12,000 tons earthenware and china).

As time went on, various branches and connections were added to the canal. The Caldon arm took the line to Leek, Froghall and, for a while, Uttoxeter. There were also short lengths at Hall Green (leaving at Hardings Wood to join the Macclesfield), Dale Hall (from Langport in Burslem), Bond End (to Burton at Shobnall), Wardle Green (which joined the T & M with the Ellesmere & Chester's Middlewich branch), the Derby Canal (from Swarkestone) and the Newcastle-under-Lyme Junction Canal which ran from the T & M at Stoke.

Although the company's funds had run perilously short towards the end of the construction stage, by June 1781 they were already in a position to pay a 5 per cent dividend. This was partly helped by the profits coming from the company's own carrying company, Hugh Henshall & Co. Tolls, and the profit on carrying rose encouragingly, especially after the through connection with the Coventry Canal (at Fradley Junction) was opened in 1790. By 1812 the annual revenues totalled £114,928, enabling the company to distribute £71,500 in dividends. By 1820, the company's debt had been completely cleared and business continued to increase. By this time, shares were changing hands at eight or nine times their face value. The success of the T & M owed much to its monopoly of the routes from Liverpool and Manchester via the Potteries to Hull and London. Jean Lindsay, however, points out that the company was also

The northern portal of Brindley's Harecastle Tunnel in 1905. The narrowboat *Westwood* and butty is preparing to go through the tunnel while the horse heads off over the hill. Northern-bound traffic, at that time, used Telford's Tunnel which is to the left of this picture

The Boat Museum archive

extremely well run, paying attention to waybills and the employment of 'walking surveyors' who kept a keen eye on the operation of the line.

By the 1820s, the company had come in for some criticism for the slightly antiquated nature of its canal. Modern waterways were broader, straighter and quicker. To offset some of this criticism and to combat some of the growing competition, the company set about a modernization programme that included doubling up some of the locks and, most expensively, building a second Harecastle Tunnel. These improvements were not enough to prevent the grievances of the canal users – who mostly complained about the small size of the boats and the lack of an alternative – or the incursion of competition. In the 1830s, that competition arrived in two forms: the Birmingham & Liverpool Junction Canal (now called the Shropshire Union) which opened in 1835 and, perhaps more importantly, the Grand Junction Railway in 1838 (which went from Birmingham to join the Liverpool to Manchester line at Newton-Le-Willows).

The T & M responded to the threats from the railway in a canal company's usual fashion. It cut tolls. But in 1845, the routes operated by the T & M were targeted directly by a proposal for four railway lines that were to become the North Staffordshire Railway (NSR). With this blanket attack, the T & M was quicker than most of the canal companies in concluding that its only option was to seek to be taken over. This it duly was on 15 January 1847, following an Act passed in June 1846.

Although one of the first actions of the NSR was to close the Uttoxeter extension of the Caldon Canal, in general the railway company started its management with some good intentions. The Act had guaranteed a certain standard of maintenance and the company reduced tolls to maintain traffic levels. It was impossible, however, to prevent the gradual loss of trade to the railway, so that although the tonnage moved by the canal stayed the same, there was a clear reduction in toll receipts. By the 1870s, receipts were under half what they had been in the 1840s and the NSR decided to concentrate its efforts on its railway business at the expense of the T & M.

This decision cannot have been helped by the high maintenance costs of certain parts of the line. Along a number of stretches in mid-Cheshire, such as around Thurlwood and Rode Heath, the vast salt mines that extend under the canal had caused a series of earth movements and canal bed collapses. This meant that the embankments, locks and bridges needed constant attention and, sometimes, complete rebuilding. The lock and bridge at Thurlwood, for example, have both been rebuilt.

Although by the second half of the nineteenth century, the days of profitable waterway transport were numbered, the trustees of the River Weaver still saw an opportunity to maintain its own traffic levels (primarily in the export of salt from the Cheshire area and the importation of coal) by a programme of improvements. One of those improvements was to develop a permanent junction with the T & M, a move which had previously been resisted by the canal company. In 1872, the trustees prepared a bill to authorise the connection via a barge lift, subsequently known as the Anderton lift. This exuberant structure was completed in 1875 and allowed movement of cargo on to the Weaver, a move which led to further loss of trade along the T & M.

By the early years of the twentieth century, the tonnage carried on the T & M was still in excess of a million tons p.a. In this respect, it remained a successful waterway and many canal-side potteries still found it cheaper to use than the railway. However, the toll receipts had declined to £45–52,000 p.a. and the company's own carrying business had been closed since 1895. There was no suggestion that the railway company had any enthusiasm for its canal business and, when in 1921 the NSR became part of the London Midland & Scottish Railway, the end of the canal as a commercial concern was definitely in sight. Toll receipts now dropped dramatically as the LMS actively sought to move traffic on to its more profitable rails. Traffic in 1940 was less than a quarter of the level thirty years before with receipts down by half despite increased tolls.

Nationalization in 1948 couldn't prevent the continuing fall off of traffic which was now under 100,000 tons p.a. In 1955, the Board of Survey on Canals and Inland Waterways reported that major improvements were needed if the T & M was to compete with other forms of transport. With increasing problems of subsidence, the maintenance of the canal was becoming more and more of a problem. The 1950s were a period of considerable losses not helped by the cessation of the gravel trade in 1958 and the salt trade in 1960. Business in the 1960s consisted mainly of the carriage of coal and of clay to the potteries. With trade disappearing completely during the late 1960s, the canal was effectively rescued by the Transport Act of 1968 when the line was designated as a cruiseway for recreational use. This it remains to this day: an important and highly popular part of the four counties ring with Harecastle Tunnel an exciting venture into the unknown.

The Walk

Start:	Stoke-on-Trent railway station (OS ref: SJ 879456)
Finish:	Kidsgrove railway station (OS ref: SJ 837544)
Distance:	8¾ miles/14 km
Map:	OS Landranger 118 (Stoke-on-Trent & Macclesfield)
Return:	Train Kidsgrove to Stoke (scarce on Sundays). Telephone: (0782) 411411. Buses also run regularly between the two towns. Telephone: (0782) 747000
Car park:	At either station
Public transport:	Stoke and Kidsgrove are both on BR main line

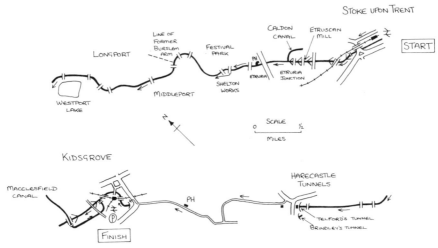

The Trent & Mersey Canal

Leave Stoke station by the main entrance and turn left and left again to pass under the railway. This leads to a superficially impenetrable roundabout. Bear left to go down an underpass which leads directly to the canal. To reach the towpath go over a bridge to the far side of the canal and turn right.

The path immediately passes under the bridges of the roundabout to reach a lock: the bottom of the Stoke flight which takes the canal up 50 ft. The lock is a typical narrow lock (7 ft in width) with a single gate at the upper pound end and a pair of mitred gates at the lower end. The second lock, with an impressive cast-iron milepost, is reached after passing under the railway.

The canal now runs adjacent to a cemetery and on to a road bridge. Here on the left at the Cliffe Vale Pottery is a once characteristic sight of the potteries: two splendid beehive kilns. Although most have been demolished or allowed to fall down, there are still a number throughout the area. The kiln is basically just a large oven in which pottery was baked in a batch process. They were coal-fired and, notoriously, belched thick smoke. Since the Second World War, the beehive has been gradually replaced by gas-fired continuous-flow ovens and these highly individual features of the landscape are steadily disappearing – much to the relief of the local environment.

Although now an area of mixed activity and dereliction, this entire length, between the Harecastle Tunnels and the southern edge of Stoke, was one that not only used the canal but whose existence was firmly based upon it. All the factories along here had their own wharf where raw materials were delivered and packed products shipped away to markets around the world. This is a part of the country therefore that didn't simply play host to a canal but which depended upon it for its industrial lifeblood. At the height of the canal age, this must have been one of the busiest sections of any inland waterway in the country. Now only a barely recognizable wharf or an overgrown factory arm remain to remind us of the role it played.

After the next lock is the tall chimney and low buildings of the Etruscan Flint and Bone Mill. This was built by Jesse Shirley in 1857 for roasting and crushing flint and bone, both of which are used as whiteners and strengtheners in ceramic pottery. The mill is served by a short arm from the canal and its raw materials and products were both shipped along the line. The mill has a museum open to visitors.

The towpath creeps up the side of the fourth lock and then shortly on to Stoke Top Lock (No. 5). Here is a British Waterways maintenance yard and, a little further on, the entrance to the Caldon Canal, a fine, almost unbelievably rural, route to Leek and Froghall (another day, another chapter).

The Shelton steelworks engulfs the Trent & Mersey Canal just north of Etruria

Continue on to a busy road bridge and the site of Wedgwood's first factory, Etruria, opened in 1769 and closed in 1950. Sadly, only two of the original buildings still stand. On the left is a building with a domed roof, now a preserved monument, even though nobody is quite sure what it was for. The bulk of the factory site is now home to a local newspaper. The site was originally at the same height as the canal but has sunk to its present level. For the other survivor of Wedgwood's time, cross the bridge and search among the newer housing for Etruria Hall, which was built in 1770 as a home for the great man within sight of his factory.

From the road bridge take the right-hand bank to pass by the Festival Basin that was built at the time of the International Garden Festival held here in 1986. The festival occupied the right-hand bank of the canal on a site that was formerly covered with blast furnaces. At the basin entrance is The China Garden pub and grill.

The vast Shelton iron- and steelworks now dominate the canal. After a railway bridge, the towpath walker becomes incorporated into the works as vast sheds overhang the entire breadth of the waterway. The complex has long lost its own production facilities (closed in 1978) but is still active as a rolling mill, as the alarming bangs and crashes signify.

Cross the second bridge (a kind of turnover bridge) after the Festival Basin to resume the walk along the left-hand bank. The right-hand side is the site of the garden festival and has been extensively landscaped. On the hill is a ski-lift for an artificial slope. The canal now bends left to go under a bridge and alongside some old tips to continue its sojourn by the steelworks. The scenery opens out as more landscape has been cleaned up, evidenced by the unexpected appearance of greenhouse tunnels on the right-hand bank.

After passing around a left-hand loop and under two bridges, we pass by a milepost and another factory to reach bridge 123. Just before the factory on the far bank is a small valley which was the course of the former Burslem Arm. More old wharves and redundant pottery factories now follow, interspersed, curiously, with a pleasant range of garden shrubs. A little further on the canal passes a splendid covered wharf, a beehive oven, a quaint yard and, when I was here, a man throwing (presumably reject) plates into a skip – all part of the famous Middleport Pottery. On the left-hand side, luckily hidden behind a high fence, the sounds of a vast tip can be heard.

Go under bridge 125 to reach Longport Wharf and bridge 126, which carries the A527 road to Burslem and Tunstall. Here are a small clutch of pubs: The Duke of Bridgwater, The Pack Horse and The Railway. If you turn right across the bridge, the Travellers Rest in Newcastle Street brew their own beer!

Just across the bridge on the right-hand bank is another beehive kiln (part of the Price & Kensington works). A few hundred yards further on, after bridge 127, the land to the left has been landscaped into the Westport Nature Reserve. A fine lake is home to a range of bird species. Interestingly, this was once home to Port Vale Football Club until subsidence rendered the ground unplayable (history does not recall how many spectators noticed).

The canal now passes under bridge 128 and bends gently left and then right in between Tunstall waterworks to the left and the gasworks to the right. There now follows a stretch yet to be reached by the restorers with some overgrown canal arms and a variety of derelict buildings and wharves. After bridge 129, the straightness of the next $\frac{1}{2}$ mile means that those with good eyesight should be able to make out the portals of the old Harecastle Tunnel. Just before reaching the tunnels, cross the canal at the turnover bridge (No. 130).

There are two canal tunnels at Harecastle: Brindley's original on the left and Telford's 'new' tunnel on the right. Brindley's, 2,880 yd long, was started on 27 July 1766 but wasn't open for another 11 years. There were problems with

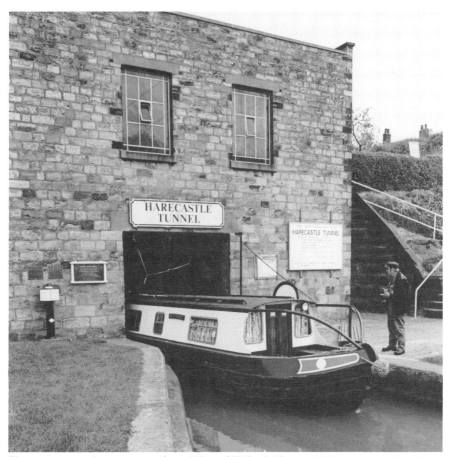

The southern portal and extractor-fan building of Telford's Harecastle Tunnel on the Trent & Mersey Canal

quicksand, hard rocks, springs of water and methane gas. Progress was only possible with the aid of a windmill for ventilation and an improved Newcomen engine for pumping out the flood waters. When it was finally opened, it was hailed as the eighth wonder of the world. Pleasure-boats took sightseers to admire it, often accompanied by bands playing music. For most of its way the tunnel is lined and arched with brick; the only exception being a 500 yd stretch of solid rock near the middle. As on the Bridgewater Canal, the length is littered with side-tunnels which burrow their way into the coal seams that were discovered during the course of the excavation.

Narrowboats were taken through the tunnel by the cumbersome process of 'legging'. The system was worked by groups of men who occupied a hut at the entrance. To push their way through, the leggers lay on their backs on the top of the narrowboat with their feet pressed against the sides of the tunnel. They then simply walked the boat to the other end, a process that could, apparently, take two to three hours. For this, the leggers received 1s. 6d. and some very tired legs.

From the outset there were problems with the quality of the tunnel and constant grievance at the time taken to pass through it. By the 1820s the situation was so bad that John Rennie was called in to try and improve matters. He agreed that the brickwork and mortar were in a poor state and that the line was crooked and difficult to navigate. Although he made a number of alternative suggestions, his recommendation was to build a new tunnel.

Sadly, Rennie died before he could start the work and Thomas Telford was employed in his place. Telford's new, 2,926 yd long, tunnel was built to the east of the old tunnel (i.e. to its right as it is looked at) and about 25 yd away from it. The intention was to pass through undisturbed ground where possible. Telford's tunnel is taller and wider than Brindley's and originally included a towpath. It took just three years to build and was opened on 30 April 1827. Telford was very pleased with it and described it as 'quite perfect'. One boatman, asked what he thought of the new tunnel, is said to have replied 'I only wish that it reached all the way to Manchester'. With two tunnels in operation, movement along the canal was much faster with each tunnel becoming one-way: north through the Telford and south through the Brindley.

In 1891, the North Staffordshire Railway provided steam tugs to tow boats through the tunnel. In 1914, the steam tug was replaced by an electric one (firstly it hauled a battery boat and then it was run by picking up current from overhead wires). This remained in operation until 1954. Brindley's tunnel, however, had sunk so much because of the various mine workings that by the First World War it was abandoned and has been shut ever since.

Nowadays a keeper is on duty at each end of the Telford Tunnel to manage the passage of leisure traffic. An average time for travelling the entire length is about fifty minutes. The brick-built, box-like structure around the entrance houses extractor fans. It was installed in 1954 to help keep the line clear of diesel fumes. The loud whirring sound of the fans only ceases when the apparatus is turned off to allow boats to enter or leave. As Telford's tunnel has also sunk, the head room along some stretches has been reduced to about 6 ft. In fact, the tunnel needs a considerable amount of maintenance and remains liable to subsidence or falls of roof lining. It was closed for four years in the 1970s (during which time the towpath was removed to make more room) and although now in good condition, it must remain a concern to British Waterways.

To reach the northern end of the tunnels, walkers have to follow the route previously taken by the barge horses while their boats were legged through below. It's not an exciting route so if someone offers you a lift, take it. Who knows you may get a chance to see the ghost of the woman who is said to have been murdered halfway along.

Those without a lift should take the steps on the right up to Chatterley Road and turn left. As the road bends sharp left, cross to Holywall Lane and then take the small road left. This passes a terrace of houses (with some very 'yappy' dogs) and steadily climbs for about a ½ mile before bending left to pass by a caravan site. An unmade road then continues to a farmyard. At what amounts to a T-junction, turn right along a metalled lane. This is Boathorse Road which bends and curves to reach a small group of houses and the Rifleman pub. From there the road gradually descends into the outskirts of Kidsgrove. Keep on this course, past some pleasant housing to reach a bend in a wide and busy road. Cross this road and bear right. Within 20 yd, a signpost points left towards the Harecastle Tunnels. After five to ten yards, turn right to go down a tree-lined track. This eventually leads to the northern entrance of Brindley's tunnel and then around to Telford's where the bright orange colour of the canal water comes as a bit of a shock. This isn't some new kind of pollution. It's caused by the presence of iron salts that have been leached from the rocks exposed along the length of the tunnel.

The towpath shortly passes under a turnover bridge and a rail bridge. Kidsgrove station can be reached by going up some steps to the left. Before finishing, however, there are still sights to see. Carry on along the path for about a ¼ mile to Hardings Wood Junction, the entrance to the Macclesfield Canal. Go over the roving bridge to pass a double lock, the first of the Red Bull Locks. This and the other double locks to be seen along this stretch were originally single but were doubled up in the 1820s as part of the attempt to speed up the flow of traffic. Cross both channels at the downstream end towards the Tavern, to pass under the road bridge and onto the second Red Bull Lock which is dominated by the sight of Pool Lock Aqueduct. This carries the Macclesfield Canal over the T & M and on to Macclesfield, Congleton and Marple where it meets the Peak Forest Canal. The entire length of this canal is open to walkers and is covered in *Canal Walks: North*.

Cross both channels using the lock's cantilevered bridges and take the thin track which passes up to the Macclesfield Canal. Turn left to pass a boatyard and then around a gentle bend to reach the roving bridge at Hardings Wood Junction. From there turn right, across the bridge, to return to Kidsgrove station.

Further Explorations

The Trent & Mersey is walkable along its entire length and thus holds out the possibility of a 93 mile long-distance footpath which could be tackled over a period of a week. The walk might start at Shardlow (on the A6 south-east of Derby) with nights at: Burton-on-Trent, Rugeley, Stone, Kidsgrove, Middle-wich, Anderton/Northwich and then on to Runcorn (along the Bridgewater Canal).

However, those who think of a long-distance walk as being under a mile, should head for the small village of Anderton, just a couple of miles to the north of Northwich in Cheshire. Anderton can be found on OS Landranger 118 at ref SJ 647752. If you take the small side road off Anderton main street (opposite the general stores and post office), you will shortly arrive at a car park near the Stanley Arms pub. Here is the Trent & Mersey Canal quietly and unobtrusively going on its way to Preston Brook. But beyond is the loud noise of the Anderton lift.

There is nothing else like it on the British canal system. The rusting bones that constitute the Anderton lift was once the connecting link between the T & M and the Weaver Navigation some 50 ft below. If you cross the T & M you will reach a small basin and the top of the lift. Here are two 162 ft long aqueducts that pass from the basin over to the lift.

In the 1860s, there was still a relatively large amount of trade between the Weaver Navigation and the Potteries via the T & M. As there was no physical link at that time, cargo was transhipped using chutes and tramways, the remnants of which can still be seen as you walk down the footpath to the lower basin. Edward Leader Williams, engineer to the Weaver, proposed a lift and Edwin Clark designed it. It was opened in 1875.

Having traversed the aqueduct, boats were loaded into a caisson, effectively a water-tight tank measuring 75 ft by 15 ft by 5 ft capable of holding two narrowboats. The tanks were originally supported on hydraulic rams and connected so that when one tank was down the other was up. To get the system moving, the opened ends of the caissons were sealed and 15 tons of water (6 in depth) was removed from the bottom tank. As the weight of the upper caisson forced it downwards, so hydraulic pressure pushed the lower tank upwards. The final push was powered by a steam engine. At the top, the 6 in of water were then restored to the caisson and the gates opened.

In a series of alterations in the early part of the twentieth century, steam power was replaced by electric, and the hydraulic system was replaced by a series of counterbalancing weights. This meant that each caisson could be worked independently.

To see the bottom basin, take the steep path that runs down to the right of the top basin. Half-way down, the remains of one of the chutes can be clearly seen. At the bottom, ICI's Winnington Works belches steam and noise and the forlorn-looking lift looms like an inmate of the Natural History Museum.

The lift, which is a designated ancient monument, is currently in the process of restoration and funds are being raised by the Anderton Boat Lift Development Group in order to undertake the process. This will be the second time since the Second World War that restoration has been needed. In the mid-1970s, the lift was closed for two years while urgent repairs were undertaken. It closed again in 1983 and has been becoming increasingly derelict ever since. At the time of my visit, the counterbalance system had been stripped off and was lying in the nearby field. Maybe you'll have more luck.

Further Information

The Trent & Mersey Canal Society Limited was founded in 1974, incorporated in 1984 and has a Wedgwood (John) as its patron. They can be contacted at:
c/o Michael Mitchell,
34 Kennedy Avenue,
New Sawley,
Long Eaton,
Nottingham,
NG10 3GF.

For those interested in the history of the canal, there are none better than:
Lindsay, Jean, *The Trent & Mersey Canal*. David & Charles, 1979.
Hadfield, Charles, *The Canals of the West Midlands*. David & Charles, 1969.

12
THE WORCESTER & BIRMINGHAM CANAL

The Tardebigge Locks

Introduction

The Worcester & Birmingham Canal was a late entrant into the canal race and seems to have had a problematical birth and a difficult life. The intention was to produce a short cut from the River Severn at Worcester into Birmingham. This it does by a head-on assault on the south-west face of the city via a spectacular series of locks that instill themselves on the memory and lock-gear turning arms of those that attempt it. Never given the same respect as the Staffordshire & Worcestershire, the W & B offers some fine country and some good walking.

The 30 miles of the W & B start at the Gas Street Basin in central Birmingham. Here for many years was the Worcester Bar, a barrier set up between the W & B and the Birmingham Canal that prevented traffic between the two canals and which wasn't finally removed until 1815. The first stretches of the W & B pass through the leafy reaches of Edgbaston and alongside Birmingham University to Selly Oak. Here, at one time, the Dudley No. 2 Canal intersected to form a major bypass route to the Black Country, much to the annoyance of the Birmingham Canal Navigations Company. The W & B, meanwhile, continues on through the outskirts of Birmingham, via Bournville, the home of Cadbury's chocolate, to King's Norton. Here the Stratford Canal leaves the W & B to pass through an elaborate guillotine stop lock and on to Lapworth, Stratford and, eventually, London. The W & B, however, heads straight into the 2,726 yd long King's Norton or West Hill Tunnel and then around the edge of Alvechurch and into Shortwood Tunnel. Tardebigge Old Wharf was, from 1807 to 1815, the terminus of the canal, still only half-way to Worcester. But with further funds the company was able to push its way through Tardebigge Tunnel and down the famous Tardebigge flight of locks where thirty locks take the canal down 217 ft to Stoke Prior. After Stoke Works, the former site of a massive salt mine, the canal passes down the Astwood flight to the junction with the Droitwich Junction Canal at Hanbury Wharf, some 9¼ miles from the Severn at Worcester. The canal now heads through Dunhampstead Tunnel and on to the small village of Tibberton. From here, the line crawls its way through the suburbs of Worcester and on to Diglis Basin and the River Severn.

You'll talk to more people on the towpath at Tardebigge in half an hour than you will in an entire day at Gas Street. It's that kind of place. The pound between the top lock and the tunnel has become a site of pilgrimage – a place to remember that the restoration of the canal network wasn't an inevitability but was only achieved by the work of far-sighted individuals who saw the inland waterways as more than just a place to put redundant Ford Escorts. It's worth going to just for that.

History

In the 1780s the only route for canal traffic from Worcester (and hence Bristol) to Birmingham was along the, often unnavigable, River Severn to Stourport, up the Staffordshire & Worcestershire Canal to Aldersley and then, after an approximately 120° turn towards the south-east, along the Birmingham Canal and into town. Although a short cut via the Stourbridge and Dudley Canals was conceived, the shallows of the Severn would remain and the line was still not as direct as perhaps it could be.

By 1789, this fact had reached the minds of those who were preparing their wallets for canal mania. A proposal was made for a direct line to Birmingham from the Severn at Worcester via Tardebigge. It was promoted in a pamphlet, published in 1790, which pointed out that the new canal would be 30 miles shorter than the Aldersley route and 15 miles shorter than the still to be finished Stourbridge/Dudley route. It was clear, the authors claimed, that the proposed line would more than halve the cost of tolls for goods being moved from Worcester to Birmingham.

Predictably, the other canal companies, notably the Staffordshire & Worcestershire and the Birmingham, weren't supportive of the new canal and successfully fought and defeated the first bill of 1790. A second bill followed with more solid support, including active participation from Birmingham businessmen who objected to the protectionist antics of the other canal companies. As a consequence, the 1791 Act enabling the building of the Worcester & Birmingham Canal was passed, a result that was celebrated in Worcester with the ringing of bells and the lighting of bonfires.

Although the Act was successful, the rival companies obtained their pound of flesh. The Birmingham, set against a junction between the W & B and its own

In times of freezing weather boatmen were unable to move their craft and were thus unable to earn a living. In 1895, the boatmen who usually plied the W & B were forced to make collections in Worcester on behalf of the Seamen and Boatmen's Friends Society

British Waterways

canal, insisted that the two be at least 7 ft apart at Gas Street Basin, a barrier that became known as the Worcester Bar. This bit of petulance on behalf of the Birmingham was reputedly to prevent water loss from its line but in practice it forced a costly transhipment of cargo and, coincidentally of course, the payment of an extra toll. The W & B was also forced by the Act to placate the Stourbridge and Dudley Companies, the proprietor of the Lower Avon Navigation, the Droitwich Canal Company and even the Worcester Corporation, by various forms of payment or financial guarantee.

In the Act, £180,000 was deemed to be sufficient to build the new line with a further £70,000 if needed. Despite the apparently onerous commitments to its rivals, the shares were fully subscribed by July 1791. In fact, following the financial success of canals like the S & W, many W & B shares changed hands at a profit even before any work was started.

The preliminary survey for the W & B was carried out by John Snape and Josiah Clowes, with Thomas Cartwright employed as engineer to build the line. The original plan was for a broad canal so that barges from the Severn could reach Birmingham without transhipment. But by mid-1794, partly due to cost and partly because of the planned junctions with the narrow Dudley and Stratford Canals, they had decided to opt for the odd combination of broad tunnels and bridges but narrow locks.

By 30 October 1795, 3 miles of canal between the Worcester Bar and Selly Oak were open, and work on King's Norton Tunnel was underway. However, in order to ensure that mill streams to the south were not starved of water, the company had to build reservoirs to supply the summit level. This additional engineering work meant that by the end of 1795, £154,067 had already been spent and the company urgently sought to access the additional £70,000. Despite these problems, the canal reached its junction with the Stratford Canal at King's Norton in May 1796 and opened the 2,760 yd long King's Norton Tunnel on 27 March 1797. Barges of 60 and 70 tons were now able to navigate from central Birmingham to Hopwood Wharf – a distance of about $8\frac{1}{2}$ miles.

The smouldering financial difficulties now began to flare and building work was seriously affected. The situation was not improved by the fact that the treasurer, Thomas Hooper, had secreted away an estimated £13,800 of the company's funds. His resignation didn't remedy the situation and the construction work slowed to such an extent that five years on, in May 1802, the southern terminus remained at Hopwood.

In an attempt to improve matters, an Act was passed in 1804 to raise more money from existing shareholders. This action improved the short term prospects and progress was once again possible. In 1805, Cartwright was re-engaged to take the canal to Tardebigge. By March 1807, he had moved on 6 miles to a point between the Shortwood and Tardebigge Tunnels where a wharf (Tardebigge Old Wharf) was built to off-load cargo for land shipment south. This proved to be quite a success and trade was brisk. There was even a regular passenger boat running between Alvechurch and Birmingham. Spirits in the W & B had now revived and yet another Act was passed in 1808. This offered attractive terms for new money and some £168,000 was, perhaps surprisingly, raised by January 1809 with shares trading at a premium. Activity on site also appeared to be more in evidence with the next big challenge: to take the canal down the 217 ft from Tardebigge to Stoke Prior.

The original proposal for seventy six locks at Tardebigge was daunting, both in terms of the cost and in the amount of time and water that would be needed to use them. The canal engineer, William Jessop, acting as consultant, agreed that there was a potential problem with water supply at the summit. So, following a proposal from the new engineer, John Woodhouse, the company agreed to experiment with a lift system in which craft would be raised and lowered in massive tanks. By the time Tardebigge Tunnel was finished in 1810, a test rig was ready and, in the winter of 1811, the lift was run for nearly three weeks, showing itself to be quick, efficient and water saving. However, by this time the committee had grown sceptical about the robustness of lifts generally and, as

Tom Rolt spent 1,800 days at Tardebigge during the Second World War when he inspected factories for the government. Here he first met Robert Aickman and from that meeting was born the Inland Waterways Association. This picture shows Rolt on board his narrowboat, *Cressy*, at Tardebigge

Tom Rolt Archive, British Waterways

another eminent engineer, John Rennie, agreed with them, they decided to build a reduced number of locks instead.

So, from 1812, a major effort on the Tardebigge Locks was under way. Progress was encouraging and with this new investors came in. By 1814, the reservoirs at Crofton and King's Norton were ready and it had been agreed to remove the Worcester Bar (replaced with a lock in July 1815). After raising £36,000 by annuities in early 1815, the company was able to complete the construction. The basin at Diglis on the Severn below Worcester was built and the whole line of 30 miles, fifty-eight locks and five tunnels was opened on 4 December 1815. Charles Hadfield suggests that the total cost was £610,000, three-and-a-half times the original estimate.

The financial position of the company was difficult from the start. It owed large sums on annuities and loans, and it was forced to raise more from shareholders. It needed to get the traffic moving as quickly as possible and promptly reduced its tolls – a tricky matter as the S & W, Stourbridge and Dudley Canals were all doing likewise to maintain their own trade. However, things improved once the canal was fully open and trade started flowing:

industrial goods and coal to Worcester, grain, timber and agricultural products to Birmingham. In 1820, toll receipts reached £14,625 and the princely dividend of £1 per share was paid in 1821.

Receipts continued to rise as traffic, especially in salt, improved. In 1825, the company expanded its activity by leasing the Lower Avon (Tewkesbury to Evesham) in order to develop markets and look for a new route to the Midlands. By 1830, rock salt from Stoke Works had became a major cargo and receipts rose sharply. This meant that by 1836–8, average receipts reached new highs at £43,488, with dividends of £4 a share. However, the potential impact of the railway age became apparent when, with the mere threat of a line between Gloucester & Birmingham, the W & B share price fell from £105 to £75. This threat became reality in 1836 when the Birmingham & Gloucester Railway Act was passed. By October 1841, the line was open and, virtually immediately, it started taking trade from the canal. The W & B and the Birmingham were forced to reduce shipping tolls and to do away with those on coal passing over the Worcester Bar. This had its inevitable effect on dividends.

In 1847, the railway dealt a body blow to the canal by taking the lion's share of the Stoke Works salt trade. The W & B tried to respond by starting its own carrying company and by promoting the Droitwich Junction Canal to link it with Droitwich. Neither gambit was to be a success. After another toll cut in 1857, the company opened negotiations with the Oxford, Worcester & Wolverhampton Railway. The talks resulted in a proposal that the railway should lease the canal for a period of twenty-one years at a rent that would yield a dividend of 1 to 2 per cent. This move was fiercely opposed by the other canal companies who feared closure and loss of a through route for their own cargoes. Following an appeal to the Board of Trade, the arrangement was indeed rendered illegal by an Act of Parliament.

Having the lease option closed to it and unable to pay dividends, the W & B then sought, in 1864, to build a railway of its own from New Street Birmingham to King's Norton. The necessary finance was not forthcoming and the plan was dropped. It was then proposed that the canal be sold to a group of railway contractors who would themselves convert it to a railway. This idea also evaporated in the face of more fierce opposition from the other canal companies.

Trade had now reached the point where it wasn't possible to pay dividends. In 1868, with some £100,000 still owing and little or no chance to raise any further money, the receiver was called in. After further opposition to another railway proposal, the Sharpness New Docks Company offered to take over the canal, including its liabilities for the Droitwich Canals, for £6,000 p.a. or £1 per share, after converted to £150,000 of 4 per cent debentures, and the liquidation of the debt of £100,473. This offer was accepted gratefully and authorized by an Act of 1874. The new company was called, rather cumbersomely, the Sharpness New Docks & Gloucester & Birmingham Navigation Company.

Although the new company started optimistically, after only four years it was losing money and only remained solvent because of the profitability of the Gloucester & Sharpness Ship Canal. Without this, the W & B would have closed. Some additional help came to hand in 1926, when George Cadbury inaugurated a fund to provide annual subsidies against losses. In return, the Docks company agreed not to close the line for as long as the subsidies were forthcoming. The trading loss at the time was £3,605 p.a. with a subsidy averaging £1,589.

In 1939, the Droitwich lines which had been disused for many years were officially abandoned. A similar fate was proposed for the W & B after it was nationalized in 1948. In the Report of the Board of Survey for the British Transport Commission in 1955, it was proposed that either the W & B or the Staffordshire & Worcestershire be retained but not both. Somehow both survived even though the remaining commercial traffic on the W & B (coal from Cannock to Worcester, and chocolate crumb from Worcester to Bourneville) ceased in 1960 and 1961 respectively. Fortunately, the W & B was never abandoned. As we all know, the 1960s saw a great resurgence in interest in canals, not from the nation's industry but from boating enthusiasts in the age of increased leisure time. The Transport Act of 1968 listed both the W & B and the S & W as cruising waterways to be retained and maintained into the future for leisure traffic. The line is now part of the increasingly popular cruising circuit and one link of the Avon Ring: a route which includes the Lower & Upper Avon Navigations, the Stratford Canal and the River Severn.

Walk

Start and finish:	Tardebigge (OS ref: SO 997694)
Distance:	5 miles/8 km
Maps:	OS Landranger 139 (Birmingham) and 150 (Worcester & The Malverns)
Car park:	At Tardebigge room for about four cars on verge on the Redditch side of the British Waterways depot on the (minor) Finstall road
Public transport:	Regular Midland Red West buses journeying between Bromsgrove and Redditch stop at Tardebigge. They do not run on Sundays. Telephone: (0527) 72265

This walk goes from Tardebrigge to the Queen's Head pub and back again. If you prefer not to have to return along the same route, it is suggested that you start from Bromsgrove where you can take the bus to Tardebigge. From the Queen's Head continue on to Stoke Works (bridge 42 with the Boat & Railway pub)

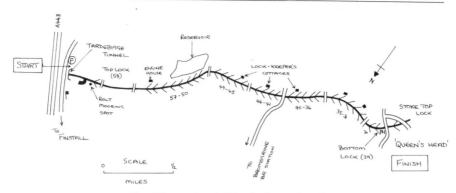

The Worcester & Birmingham Canal

from where another Midland Red West bus can convey you back to Bromsgrove. This would yield a walk of about 4 miles. However, it is clearly vital to check the times of the buses from Stoke Works using the telephone number above.

If arriving by bus at Tardebigge, continue on the road towards Redditch for approximately 50 yd to what appears to be a bridge over the canal but which is in fact the entrance to Tardebigge Tunnel. Here you'll meet those who came by car. A path leads down to the left-hand bank of the canal where, to the right, the

The southern portal of Tardebigge Tunnel

entrance to the 580 yd long tunnel can be seen. It's worth noting that this is a relatively wide tunnel for a narrow-locked canal. This wasn't a deliberate design to facilitate passage both ways but is a remnant of the original plan to make the line a barge canal. There is no towpath through the tunnel and barge horses were forced to go up to the road where they turned left and then right along a footpath which leads to the northern portal. Originally boats were taken through the tunnel by 'leggers', men who lay on their backs to push the boats through by walking against the roof. This practice was abandoned in the 1870s when company tugs were employed to pull boats through. This, in turn, was abandoned during the early part of the twentieth century. There are three more tunnels (Edgbaston, West Hill and Shortwood) between here and central Birmingham, some 14 miles to the north-east.

A few yards further on, the British Waterways' yard situated at what was once called New Wharf (Old Wharf is on the northern side of the tunnel) offers comfort to passing boaters.

The scene around Tardebigge New Wharf might seem quiet and unspectacular but it has a unique place in waterways restoration history. During most of the Second World War (for 1800 days to be exact), the author Tom Rolt and his wife Angela moored their boat *Cressy* at a point about 50 yd beyond the BW basin. Here they lived while Tom was employed by the government during the day and started on a fledgling writing career by night. In doing the latter, he had written a book that was to be a landmark in waterways restoration. *Narrow Boat* was originally published in 1944 and had almost immediately attracted the attention of Robert Aickman, a man who felt deeply for the country's waterways but who otherwise was a novice in the ways of the canals. Aickman was moved to write to Rolt to express his admiration for both the book and the motives. In response, Rolt invited Aickman and his wife, Ray, to visit *Cressy* and so, in August 1945, the four met for the first time. From that meeting the Inland Waterways Association, the premier force in the fight against the abandonment of the British canal network, was formed. To mark the spot, the Worcester & Birmingham Canal Society have erected a plinth just on the other side of the canal. Interestingly, this notes the first meeting between Rolt and Aickman as being in 1946. To reach the plinth, cross the canal at the lock.

Although the start of the IWA was inauspicious, and some of its early days a little shaky, the association has gone from strength to strength. The IWA campaigns for the restoration, retention and development of inland waterways in the British Isles and for their fullest commercial and recreational use. There are branches up and down the country with literally thousands of members contributing both directly and indirectly to the aims. New members are always welcome and the address of the association is included at the end of this book.

Even without the birth of the IWA, Rolt's descriptions of life here at Tardebigge during the Second World War would still make the place special. The goings on are wonderfully told in his autobiography *Landscape with Canals* which contains portraits of the characters who staffed the boatyard and worked the locks of what was then still, officially at least, a working waterway.

About 50 yd beyond the plinth is the start of the other reason why Tardebigge is so famous throughout the canal world. The view to the south should give a hint as to what is to come. The land in front of us and to the right falls rapidly towards the Severn Valley to offer views of the Welsh border and even the Malvern hills away in the distance. Thus Tardebigge plays host to the biggest flight of locks in the country. There are thirty of them in the Tardebigge flight proper with a total rise/fall of some 217 ft. If a further six at Stoke are included, the total rise/fall comes to 259 ft. All these locks take the W & B from what is known as the Birmingham Level (453 ft above sea level – the same height as the Birmingham Canal at Gas Street) down, through a further twenty-two locks, to the River Severn at Worcester.

Tardebigge Top Lock (No. 58), apart from being the first of the flight, also has the honour of being one of the deepest narrow locks on the system with a fall of some 14 ft. The reason for this is one of those peculiar accidents of history. When the canal was being built in the early 1790s, it was thought that the company would have to pump water for their part of the Birmingham level all the way from the Severn. To avoid this, radical answers were sought. John Woodhouse, an engineer on the Grand Junction Canal (now the Grand Union), offered to build an experimental vertical lift at Tardebigge at his own expense if the company agreed to pay for the excavation work and the masonry. The objective was to reduce the number of locks planned for the flight and to avoid excessive loss of water down the line. As a lift would use hardly any water in operation, the W & B company agreed to the experiment and so, while they still continued with the construction of reservoir capacity at the summit, Woodhouse built his lift.

The test rig was ready in June 1808. It was a 12 ft lift and was situated where the top lock is now. It consisted of a wooden tank, big enough to carry a narrowboat and weighing 64 tons fully loaded, counterbalanced by a platform full of bricks. The two sides were connected by chains passing over a set of cast-iron wheels. The canal was sealed using wooden paddles at each end of the tank which were raised or lowered to allow boats to come and go. The lift was moved by two men who wound the tank up and down. From 25 February to 16 March 1811, the lift worked solidly with a peak on 15 March, when 110 boats were raised or lowered in just twelve hours.

This performance failed to impress the W & B committee, however, who invited comments from the well-known canal engineer, John Rennie. It is true to say that such lifts did not have a good reputation for their robustness and whatever Woodhouse had achieved was almost irrelevent. Locks were a slower and more water-costly system but they were at least reliable and a known quantity. On this basis, both Rennie and the committee abandoned the idea of using lifts at Tardebigge and the test lift was dismantled. The actual site of the test rig was a slightly larger than normal drop but was converted into a single fall lock in 1815. Thus the deeper than average fall.

Our walk now passes under a neat accommodation bridge and on to bridge 55. Just beyond, by lock 57, is the Engine House, a former pumping house that is now a restaurant and night club. Originally the house contained a steam engine which pumped water from the reservoir, soon to be visible to the left of the canal, up into the Birmingham level.

As you walk down the hill, the long line of locks to the next bridge appears before you, two with neighbouring cottages. At one point there is a sudden and unexpected view over to the reservoir on the left. Just before the bridge (No. 54) a number of rough-hewn paths up the bank to the left invite the curious for a closer look at the reservoir as well as a less obstructed view to the south. In summer months, an endless string of boats with their, by now, weary crews can be seen passing up the locks, no doubt wondering when their toils will be over and dreading the return trip when the whole procedure will have to be gone through all over again.

There is now a mile of steadily changing scenery where locks, cottages and boats intermix to make a peculiarly bustling foreground in what is otherwise a rather remote and peaceful part of the world. The toil involved in negotiating the flight brings out a camaraderie among the boaters who share their experience with anybody and everybody in reach. From all the activity, it isn't

Working the Tardebigge flight of thirty locks on the Worcester & Birmingham Canal is often better to watch than to participate in!

too hard to imagine the scene here when the canal was a working one. Interestingly, boats on the W & B were often towed by donkeys, working in pairs, rather than horses. Why this should be the case isn't known.

Before long you reach Tardebigge Bottom Lock and realize that there are no more locks in front of you. It makes you feel somewhat deprived like a toddler who's had a favourite toy taken away. The line bends around slightly to the left and the canalside gardens of the Queens Head pub are seen over to the right. By taking the leafy track to the left of the next bridge (No. 48) you will reach the road. Turn right for the pub.

Here you can either meet someone kind enough to take you back to Tardebigge or you can simply about face to re-meet with all those boat crews who are still struggling up the line.

If you plan to go on to Stoke Works for the Bromsgrove bus, continue along the left-hand bank of the canal, past six locks to Stoke Wharf, a pleasant spot with a warehouse, some cottages, a crane and the Navigation pub. Another $\frac{1}{2}$ mile will take you past the remnants of an enormous salt works (now a pharmaceutical factory) to Stoke Works. The salt mines here once brought a considerable amount of trade to the canal but are now long gone. To reach the bus stop, you should turn off right at bridge 42 near the Boat & Railway pub (OS map 150, ref: SO 944663).

Further Explorations

The richness of public transport between Worcester and Droitwich should tempt some to devise a walk between the two towns, a distance of approximately 12 miles. Use OS Landranger 150 (Worcester & The Malverns).

From the Market Hall car park in the centre of Droitwich, cross the road to find the fine barge lock which actually has a swing bridge halfway along it. Those interested in this particular kind of oddity will find a similar structure at Hungerford Marsh Lock on the Kennet & Avon Canal. This lock marks the beginning of the Droitwich Barge Canal that goes south-west from here to join the River Severn near Hawford. This in itself is worthy of further exploration and those with the time and inclination can turn left to follow the public footpath for 6 miles to the River Severn. The barge canal was opened in 1771 having been surveyed by James Brindley no less. The route was an important route for Droitwich salt. By the Second World War, the line was officially abandoned but, with the formation of the Droitwich Canals Trust in 1973, it is being gradually improved throughout.

Towpathers to Worcester will, however, not be so distracted and should turn right at the barge lock to join the River Salwarpe and on to a small, ornate road bridge. Go up to the road and bear right along the A38 to traffic lights and turn left on to the B4090. This is the Salt Way.

The road continues on to a point where it passes under the M5 motorway. Just before the motorway, the River Salwarpe, which has been on the left-hand side of the road, deviates northwards. From this point, the Droitwich Junction Canal was built with seven locks in 1851 to provide the salt town of Droitwich with a direct link to Birmingham via the W & B. The DJC fell into disuse in the 1920s and was officially abandoned in July 1939. However, in recent years there have been moves to restore the line and it is now owned by the Droitwich Borough Council. By dodging right along lanes off the Salt Way, traces of the old line can be seen running parallel with the road. After a while, you need dodge no longer as various moored boats indicate that the line is intact and in water.

The Salt Way crosses the W & B at Hanbury Wharf where the Eagle & Sun offers refreshment. Towpathers to Worcester should cross the canal and turn right to pass along the left-hand bank of the line. After nearly 2 miles, the canal goes through Dunhampstead Tunnel where walkers have to deviate off to the left and over the hill, returning to the canal at bridge 30. From there the canal winds through Tibberton (opportunity here for lunch and/or some shopping) before going under the M5 and down the six Offerton Locks.

By now the outskirts of Worcester are making themselves evident and the canal goes down a further six locks to skirt Worcester City football ground where the towpath changes sides. From there, the canal slips quietly through the town. Bridge 10 is a splendidly arched and extrovertly 'holed' railway bridge just before Lowesmoor Wharf. Re-cross the canal at bridge 5 and continue on past two more locks and into Diglis Basin.

Diglis isn't as grand as Stourport but has similar intent. Beyond the wide basin, the dry dock and the two massive barge locks, lies the River Severn. Turn right here to take the river path round to the main river bridge. If you turn right here you will reach firstly the bus station (both Midlands Red West (No. 144) and Citibus (No. 22) offer services to Droitwich) or Foregate Street station from where trains compete for your return trip.

The proximity of train and canal at the Birmingham end also allows an easy one-way walk between New Street station and Bournville; a distance of about 5 miles. To reach Gas Street Basin from New Street follow the instructions given under Further Explorations of the Birmingham Canal Navigations. Cross the Worcester Bar (where the W & B joins the BCN) and turn left to take the right-hand side of the canal. Within a short distance the line crosses a small aqueduct and turns abruptly right. Our course is now due south and we pass through the leafy suburbs of Edgbaston including, for a time on the right, the Botanical Gardens and, on the left, the campus of Birmingham University. After passing under a railway bridge, the canal reaches Selly Oak. At bridge 79A, the railway re-crosses. Three bridges further on, pass up to the road and turn right to reach Bournville station. Before returning to New Street, you might consider visiting the Cadbury World visitor centre in the nearby chocolate factory. How can you resist?

Further Information

The address of the Worcester & Birmingham Canal Society is:
    1 Southwold Close,
    St Peter the Great,
    Worcester,
    Worcestershire,
    WR5 3RD.

The history of the W&B can be traced through the pages of:
Hadfield, Charles, *The Canals of the West Midlands*. David & Charles, 1969.

Tom Rolt's account of Tardebigge during the Second World War and his account of the birth of the Inland Waterways Association can be found in:
Rolt, L.T.C., *Landscape with Canals*. Alan Sutton Publishing, 1977.

A more independent history of the IWA and a fascinating account of how the country's waterways were saved can be found in:
Bolton, David, *Race Against Time*. Mandarin Paperbacks, 1990.

APPENDIX A

General Reading

This book can, of course, only provide you with a brief glimpse of the history and workings of the waterway network. Other authors are far more qualified than I to fill the gaps and the following reading matter may help those who wish to know more.

Magazines

There are two monthly canal magazines that are available in most newsagents: *Canal & Riverboat* and *Waterways World*. Towpathers may be particularly interested in *Waterways World* as it has a monthly canal walks column.

Books

There are a wide range of canal books available, varying between guides for specific waterways to learned historical texts. There should be something for everyone's level of interest, taste and ability to pay. Libraries also carry a good stock of the more expensive works and are well worth a visit.

All the books listed here are available in paperback unless marked with an asterisk.

For a good general introduction to canals that won't stretch the intellect, or the pocket, too far:
Smith, P.L., *Discovering Canals in Britain*. Shire Books, 1984.
Burton, A. and Platt, D., *Canal*. David & Charles, 1980.
Hadfield, C., *Waterways sights to see*. David & Charles, 1976.*
Rolt, L.T.C., *Narrowboat*. Methuen, 1944.

This can be taken a few steps further with the more learned:
Hadfield, C., *British Canals*. David & Charles, 1984; new edition Alan Sutton, 1993.

There are a number of books that are predominantly collections of old photographs. Two examples are:
Ware, M., *Canals and Waterways*, History in Camera Series. Shire Books, 1987.
Gladwin, D., *Building Britain's Canals*. K.A.F. Brewin Books, 1988.

At least three companies publish boating guides:
Nicholson's Guides to the Waterways. Three volumes.
Pearson's Canal & River Companions. Eight volumes (so far).
Waterways World. Eight volumes (so far).
Of the three, Pearson's guides are the most useful for towpathers, with their volume on the Birmingham Canal Navigations heading the list. The only problem for users is the duplication between volumes. Other Pearson volumes applicable to Midlands canals are:
Four Counties Ring, Midlands Ring, Severn & Avon (Avon Ring), *Shropshire Union & Llangollen Canals, South Midlands & Warwickshire Ring*.

APPENDIX B

Useful Addresses

British Waterways

BW are the guardians of the vast majority of the canal network and deserve our support. There are offices all over the country but their customer services department can be found at:

British Waterways,
Greycaine Road,
Watford,
WD2 4JR.
Telephone: (0923) 226422

Inland Waterways Association

The IWA was the first, and is still the premier, society that campaigns for Britain's waterways. They publish a member's magazine, *Waterways*, and provide various services. There are numerous local groups which each hold meetings, outings, rallies, etc. Head office is at:

Inland Waterways Association,
114 Regent's Park Road,
London,
NW1 8UQ.
Telephone: (071) 5862556

Towpath Action Group

The Towpath Action Group campaigns for access to and maintenance of the towpaths of Britain and publish a regular newsletter. They are thus the natural home of all keen towpathers.

Towpath Action Group,
23 Hague Bar Road,
New Mills,
Stockport,
SK12 3AT.

APPENDIX C

Museums

A number of canal museums are springing up all over the country. The following are within reach of the area covered within this book and are wholly devoted to canals or have sections of interest:

MUSEUM OF SCIENCE AND
INDUSTRY
Newhall Street,
Birmingham,
B3 1RZ.
Telephone: (021) 2351661

BLACK COUNTRY MUSEUM
Tipton Road,
Dudley,
West Midlands,
DY1 4SQ
Telephone: (021) 5579643

THE BOAT MUSEUM
Dockyard Road,
Ellesmere Port,
South Wirral,
L65 4EF
Telephone: (051) 3555017

THE NATIONAL WATERWAYS
MUSEUM
Llanthony Warehouse,
Gloucester Docks,
Gloucester,
GL1 2EH
Telephone: (0452) 307009

THE CANAL MUSEUM
Stoke Bruerne,
Towcester,
Northamptonshire,
NN12 7SE
Telephone: (0604) 862229

INDEX